MW00565268

Living in the
Mingled Spirit
for the Reality
of the
Body of Christ

The Holy Word for Morning Revival

Witness Lee

Living Stream Ministry
Anaheim, CA • www.lsm.org

First Edition, December 2006.

ISBN 0-7363-3334-7

Published by

Living Stream Ministry

2431 W. La Palma Ave., Anaheim, CA 92801 U.S.A.

P. O. Box 2121, Anaheim, CA 92814 U.S.A.

Printed in the United States of America

06 07 08 09 10 11 12 / 10 9 8 7 6 5 4 3 2 1

Contents

Preface

1. This book is intended as an aid to believers in developing a daily time of morning revival with the Lord in His word. At the same time, it provides a limited review of the Thanksgiving weekend conference held in Washington, D.C., November 23-26, 2006. The subject of the conference was "Living in the Mingled Spirit for the Reality of the Body of Christ." Through intimate contact with the Lord in His word, the believers can be constituted with life and truth and thereby equipped to prophesy in the meetings of the church unto the building up of the Body of Christ.

2. The content of this book is taken primarily from the conference message outlines, the text and footnotes of the Recovery Version of the Bible, selections from the writings of Witness Lee and Watchman Nee, and *Hymns,* all of which are published by Living Stream Ministry.

3. The book is divided into weeks. One conference message is covered per week. Each week presents first the message outline, followed by six daily portions, a hymn, and then some space for writing. The message outline has been divided into days, corresponding to the six daily portions. Each daily portion covers certain points and begins with a section entitled "Morning Nourishment." This section contains selected verses and a short reading that can provide rich spiritual nourishment through intimate fellowship with the Lord. The "Morning Nourishment" is followed by a section entitled "Today's Reading," a longer portion of ministry related to the day's main points. Each day's portion concludes with a short list of references for further reading and some space for the saints to make notes concerning their spiritual inspiration, enlightenment, and enjoyment to serve as a reminder of what they have received of the Lord that day.

4. The space provided at the end of each week is for composing a short prophecy. This prophecy can be composed by considering all of our daily notes, the "harvest" of our

inspirations during the week, and preparing a main point with some sub-points to be spoken in the church meetings for the organic building up of the Body of Christ.

5. Following the last week in this volume, we have provided reading schedules for both the Old and New Testaments in the Recovery Version with footnotes. These schedules are arranged so that one can read through both the Old and New Testaments of the Recovery Version with footnotes in two years.

6. As a practical aid to the saints' feeding on the Word throughout the day, we have provided verse cards at the end of the volume, which correspond to each day's scripture reading. These may be removed and carried along as a source of spiritual enlightenment and nourishment in the saints' daily lives.

7. The conference message outlines were compiled by Living Stream Ministry from the writings of Witness Lee and Watchman Nee. The outlines, footnotes, and references in the Recovery Version of the Bible are by Witness Lee. All of the other references cited in this publication are from the published ministry of Witness Lee and Watchman Nee.

Thanksgiving Weekend Conference
(November 23-26, 2006)

General Subject:

Living in the Mingled Spirit
for the Reality of the Body of Christ

Banners:

God's unique purpose is to mingle Himself with us
so that He becomes our life, nature, and content
and so that we become His corporate expression.

The mingled spirit is the unique organ
for us to live the life of a God-man and
for God to bring forth and build up
the Body of Christ.

We must be filled with the beautifying,
bride-preparing Spirit mingled with our spirit
so that we can be prepared to be
Christ's glorious church, His beautiful bride, and
the house of God's beauty for God's expression.

We must experience the slaying Spirit
mingled with our spirit
so that everything of God's adversary
can be killed within us,
enabling us to rule in the divine life of the Spirit
over Satan, sin, and death for God's dominion.

The Mingled Spirit and the Body of Christ

Scripture Reading: Rom. 8:4; 12:4-5; 1 Cor. 6:17; 12:12-13, 27; Eph. 2:22; 4:16

Day 1 I. **God's unique purpose is to mingle Himself with us so that He becomes our life, our nature, and our content and so that we become His corporate expression (John 14:20; 15:4-5; Eph. 3:16-21; 4:4-6, 16):**

A. The mingling of God and man is an intrinsic union of the elements of divinity and humanity to form one organic entity, yet the elements remain distinct in the union.

B. The will of God is the mingling of God with man, and the fulfillment of God's eternal purpose depends on the mingling of divinity and humanity (1:5, 9; 3:11).

C. The Lord Jesus Christ is the mingling of God and man (Luke 1:31-35).

D. The Christian life is the mingling of divinity and humanity; to be a Christian means to be mingled with God, to be a God-man (2 Tim. 3:17):

1. In His economy God mingles Himself with us to become one entity with us (1 Cor. 6:17).

2. We may be saved to the extent that we and God are completely mingled as one, having one life and one living (John 15:4-5; Gal. 2:20; Phil. 1:19-21a).

Day 2 E. The Body of Christ is the enlargement of Christ, the enlargement of the One who is the mingling of God and man (Eph. 1:22-23; 4:16):

1. We need to understand the Body of Christ from the perspective of the mingling of divinity and humanity (vv. 4-6).

2. In the Gospels the mingling of God and man produced the Head; in Acts the enlargement of the mingling of God and man produced the Body of Christ (Eph. 1:22-23; 4:15-16).

3. In Ephesians 4:4-6 four persons—the Body,
the Spirit, the Lord, and God the Father—
are actively mingled together:
   a. The Father is embodied in the Son, the
   Son is realized as the Spirit, and the
   Spirit is mingled with the believers.
   b. This mingling is the constitution of the
   Body of Christ.
4. The processed and consummated Triune
God mingles Himself with His chosen
people in their humanity, and this mingling
is the genuine oneness of the Body of Christ
(v. 3; John 17:21-23).
F. The true meaning of building is that God is
building Himself into man and building man
into Himself; this is the mingling of God and
man (Eph. 2:21-22).
G. The New Jerusalem will be the ultimate consummation of the mingling of God and man
(Rev. 21:2).

Day 3 II. **We need to see a vision of the mingled
spirit—the divine Spirit mingled with our
regenerated human spirit (1 Cor. 6:17; Rom.
8:4):**
A. The Father is in the Son, the Son is the Spirit,
and the Spirit is now mingled with our spirit (John
14:9-10, 16-18; 1 Cor. 15:45b; 6:17; Rom. 8:16).
B. The union of God and man is a union of the two
spirits, the Spirit of God and the spirit of man
(1 Cor. 2:11-16); the union of these two spirits
is the deepest mystery in the Bible.
C. The focus of God's economy is the mingled spirit, the divine Spirit mingled with the human
spirit; whatever God intends to do or accomplish is related to this focus (Eph. 3:9, 5; 1:17;
2:22; 3:16; 4:23; 5:18; 6:18).
D. The mingled spirit is both the Spirit of the Lord
and our spirit (Rom. 8:4; 2 Cor. 3:17; 1 Cor. 15:45b;
6:17).

E. The mingled spirit is a spirit that is one spirit
with God and that is the same as God in His life
and nature but not in His Godhead (1 John 5:11;
2 Pet. 1:4):

1. The divine Spirit and the human spirit are
mingled as one within us so that we can
live the life of a God-man, a life that is God
yet man and man yet God (Gal. 2:20; Phil.
1:19-21a).

2. The God-man living is the living of the two
spirits, the Spirit of God and the spirit of
man, joined and mingled together as one
(1 Cor. 6:17).

Day 4   F. The mingled spirit is the key to the Christian
life (Rom. 8:4; Eph. 2:22).

G. To be proper Christians, we must know that
the Lord Jesus today, as the embodiment of the
Triune God, is the Spirit indwelling our spirit
and is mingled with our spirit as one spirit (2 Cor.
3:17; 1 Cor. 15:45b; 6:17).

H. By being one spirit with the Lord, we can experience Christ as the all-inclusive One and take
Him as everything (1:2, 24, 30; 2:8, 10; 3:11;
5:7-8; 10:3-4; 11:3; 12:12; 15:20, 45, 47).

I. God's unique requirement of us as believers is
that we live and walk by the Spirit in our spirit
(Gal. 5:16, 25; 6:18).

J. Ultimately, the Bible requires only one thing of
us—that we walk according to the mingled
spirit (Rom. 8:4):

1. The key to everything in the Christian life
is found in the wonderful Spirit who is in
our regenerated spirit and who has become
one spirit with our spirit (Phil. 1:19; 4:23;
2 Tim. 4:22).

Day 5   2. To live in the spirit is to let Christ fill and
saturate us until He permeates our whole
being and is thereby expressed through us
(Eph. 2:22; 3:16-21).

Day 6 **III. The Body of Christ is absolutely a matter in the mingled spirit; thus, to be in the reality of the Body of Christ is to be in the mingled spirit and to live in the mingled spirit (Rom. 8:4-6; 12:4-5; 1 Cor. 6:17; 12:12-13, 27):**

A. The church as the Body of Christ is a group of people who allow God to be mingled with them and who are mingled with God (Eph. 3:16-21).

B. The reality of the Body of Christ is a corporate living by the God-men, who are united, mingled, and constituted together with God by the mingling of humanity with divinity and divinity with humanity (4:1-6, 15-16).

C. In actuality and practicality, the Body of Christ is the mingled spirit (1 Cor. 12:12-13, 27; 6:17):

  1. The Body of Christ is the corporate Christ composed of the Head and the Body with many members; this corporate Christ is the mingled spirit (12:12; 6:17).

  2. To live, act, and move in the mingled spirit is to live, act, and move in the Body of Christ (Rom. 8:4, 14; 12:4-5).

  3. To be in the mingled spirit is to be the Body of Christ actually and practically (1 Cor. 6:17; 12:27).

Morning Nourishment

Eph.   **Predestinating us unto sonship through Jesus Christ**
1:5   **to Himself, according to the good pleasure of His will.**
John   **In that day you will know that I am in My Father, and**
14:20   **you in Me, and I in you.**

When we speak of God's will, we must trace it to the desire of His heart. Ephesians 1:5-12 is...concerning the will of God. It says that God in eternity has a plan, which is according to His good pleasure....To attain His pleasure, He has a plan which He purposed to fulfill to reach His goal. This purpose is His will.

Since God's will is His heart's desire, we must learn what that desire is. It is the mingling of God with man. To mingle with man is both God's desire and His will....God in eternity planned according to His heart's desire to attain the goal of mingling Himself with man. God...has this one will: to work Himself into man and to mingle Himself with man. His creation, redemption, sanctification, and all other aspects of His work are for this one purpose. This is the one desire of His heart in the universe; it is the only goal, and it is the basic principle of all His work in the New Testament. Therefore, if we desire to know God's will in any situation, we must first ascertain whether the situation is conducive to the mingling of Himself with us. Without this mingling, no matter how good or praiseworthy the situation may be, it is not God's will.

The earthly life of our Lord Jesus is the perfect expression of this principle. The Lord said, "Behold, I have come...to do Your will" (Heb. 10:7, 9), and, "I do not seek My own will but the will of Him who sent Me" (John 5:30)....[The Lord's] entire life on this earth was God's will. However, He also said, "The words that I say to you I do not speak from Myself, but the Father who abides in Me does His works" (John 14:10). This means that while He was on this earth, His words, His deeds and all His living did not originate from Himself, but the Father, who was abiding in Him, mingled with Him and worked through Him. From these three Scripture quotations we see that the Lord's life on this earth was in obedience to God's will and that it was a life of the mingling of God with man. (*The Experience of Life*, pp. 159-161)

Today's Reading

The incarnation of Christ simply means the mingling of God with humanity. Mingling is much more than mixing together; it is an intrinsic union. In the entire history of mankind such a thing had never occurred. For four thousand years, God was God and man was man. Yes, man had something to do with God, and God sometimes made contact with man; yet the two remained separate. However, when Christ was born as a man,…a child was born… who was called the Mighty God (Isa. 9:6).…The Almighty God… mingle[d] Himself with a man.…This was accomplished in Jesus Christ, and this is the very desire of God for you and me—that He be mingled with us. (*The Four Major Steps of Christ*, pp. 6-7)

The believers are children of God. This implies regeneration, the new birth. To be a child of God means that we have been born of God.…When we were born of God in our spirit, we were mingled with Him. Conception always precedes birth.…This involves even more than mingling.…He has been conceived within us, and we have been born of Him to become His children.

Now that we have been born of God, we need to eat Him and drink Him. To be sure, whatever we eat and digest is assimilated by us and mingled with us.…The Lord clearly likened Himself to food for us to eat, digest, and assimilate. Those who oppose the teaching that believers are mingled with God are short of the proper knowledge. They do not realize that at the time of our conversion, God was conceived within us, and we were born of Him. At that time, we and God, humanity and divinity, were joined in a marvelous way. After our spiritual birth, we need to feed on God day by day.…When we take in the Triune God as our food and drink, He is mingled with us, and we are mingled with Him. (*Life-study of Philippians*, pp. 111-112)

Further Reading: The Experience of Life, ch. 8; *Life-study of Luke*, msg. 3; *The Four Major Steps of Christ*, chs. 1-2; *The Conclusion of the New Testament*, msg. 26; *Living in the Spirit*, ch. 3

Enlightenment and inspiration: _____

_____

_____

_____

Morning Nourishment

Eph. And He subjected all things under His feet and gave
1:22-23 Him *to be* Head over all things to the church, which
is His Body, the fullness of the One who fills all in all.
Col. ...Holding the Head, out from whom all the Body,
2:19 being richly supplied and knit together by means of
the joints and sinews, grows with the growth of God.

The church is the enlargement of the mingling of God and
man, the enlargement of Christ. If there is no mingling of God
with man and man with God, there can be no church. Though
many believers have God's life in them, this mingling is not seen
in their living; the practical expression of the mingling of God and
man is not among them. I believe it is easier for us to understand
the Body of Christ from the perspective of the mingling of God
and man. We may be genuinely saved, zealously serving the Lord,
and diligently caring for the church, but the mingling of God and
man may not be present within us. Many children of God preach
the gospel zealously, but the mingling of God and man is not present within them; instead, man's zeal and diligence are present.
They preach the gospel out of themselves; the element of God is
not in their gospel preaching. They may even speak of God while
they preach, but in their actions and speech there is only man's
element, not God's. (*The Church as the Body of Christ*, pp. 60-61)

Today's Reading

God came to the earth to be mingled with man, in the man
Jesus Christ. Hence, Jesus Christ is the beginning of the mingling
of God and man. This mingling made the production of the Body
of Christ, which is the church, possible. Christ is the Head of the
Body, the church. The church is the enlargement of the principle
of God being mingled with man. This enlargement results in the
Body of Christ.

In the Gospels, the mingling of God and man produced the
Head, Christ. In Acts, the enlargement of the mingling of God and
man produced the Body of Christ....The first five books of the
New Testament show a clear picture of a great person. The four

Gospels show this great person, and the book of Acts shows the enlargement of this great person.

We need to connect Acts with the Gospels to see a complete man, the Head and the Body. This man is a mysterious, universal man, who is God yet man and man yet God. He is also the mingling of divinity and humanity....In Acts Christ as the Head is in the heavens, but the Body He produced is on earth. We need spiritual eyes to see that this great person as the Head is in the heavens and that His Body is on earth. However, the Head is not separate from the Body; rather, in this universe they are connected from the heavens to the earth and from the earth to the heavens. The book of Acts is a record of the enlargement and continuation of the mingling of God and man. Christ is not a person with a group of associates; He is the Head with a Body. (*The Church as the Body of Christ,* pp. 59-60)

The entire Scriptures reveal these two works of God, the work of creation and the work of building God into man and man into God. The building of God is the mingling of divinity with humanity. Therefore, at the end of the Scriptures there is a city as the building of God, and that city is the mingling of God with all the redeemed persons...composed together as a container to contain God and be mingled and permeated with God. This is the mingling of God and man as the building of God.

The New Jerusalem is a full picture of the mingling of the Triune God with His redeemed creatures, the mingling of divinity with humanity. Now God is no longer merely a God outside of man. He is a God within man. (*The Building of God,* pp. 15-16, 12)

Further Reading: The Church as the Body of Christ, ch. 5; *The Building of God,* chs. 1-2; *The Practical Way to Live a Life according to the High Peak of the Divine Revelation in the Holy Scriptures,* ch. 6; *The Central Line of the Divine Revelation,* msg. 28; *God's New Testament Economy,* msg. 28; *Crystallization-study of the Gospel of John,* msg. 14; *The God-men,* ch. 4; *The Vision of God's Building,* chs. 16-17

Enlightenment and inspiration: _____
_____
_____
_____

Morning Nourishment

Rom. **The Spirit Himself witnesses with our spirit that**
8:16 **we are children of God.**
1 Cor. **But he who is joined to the Lord is one spirit.**
6:17

The regenerated spirit of the believers and the consummated Spirit of God are mingled as one spirit (1 Cor. 6:17)…within us so that we can live a God-man life, a life that is God yet man and man yet God. Hence, the God-man life is a living of the two spirits, the Spirit of God and the spirit of man, joined and mingled together as one.

The union of God and man is altogether a matter of the union of [these] two spirits.…God is Spirit and man has a spirit; thus, these two spirits can be united together as one.

The union of the Spirit of God and the spirit of the believers brings God into man that God and man may be joined and mingled together. This causes divinity and humanity to be blended as one, yet without producing a third nature. This is the crucial significance of joining and mingling. This thought is very deep. This is something that the Lord has shown us in His recovery. (*The Issue of the Union of the Consummated Spirit of the Triune God and the Regenerated Spirit of the Believers,* pp. 30, 34, 36)

Today's Reading

The key of God's organic salvation is the Spirit Himself with our spirit [Rom. 8:16].…The Spirit Himself with our spirit is doing one thing: witnessing that we are the children of God.…After regeneration the regenerating Spirit remains in our regenerated spirit and mingles Himself with our spirit to make the two one [1 Cor. 6:17].

Not only are we God-men but also we are one with God, one spirit with God. The human spirit and the divine Spirit are not only joined and mingled but are also one spirit.…God is the Spirit and in His marvelous organic salvation, He has made us one spirit with Him.…Our real status is that we are one spirit with God. We have been saved to such a high level. What God is, we are.…When we realize our status, this will affect our living.

According to 1 Corinthians 6:17 God's intention in His organic salvation is to join the believer's spirit with His Spirit as one spirit—a mingled spirit. Eventually, this is not just the mingled spirit but a spirit that is one spirit with God, that is the same as God in His life and nature but not in His Godhead. This is the key to open the eight sections of the organic salvation of God. (*The Divine and Mystical Realm,* pp. 53-54)

Now we have not only the divine Spirit in our spirit but also the mingling of the divine Spirit with our spirit [Rom. 8:16; 1 Cor. 6:17]. Thus, the two spirits are one....Praise the Lord that these two spirits have been mingled into one spirit! This is the reason that in the verses concerning our walk in the spirit, it is difficult for the translators to determine whether to render *pneuma* as "Spirit" or as "spirit." Actually, to walk according to the Spirit means to walk according to both the divine Spirit and the human spirit, according to the two spirits mingled as one. The two spirits are mingled not in the heavens nor outside of us but within us. This is the focus of the divine economy. Whatever God intends to do or accomplish is related to this focus. If we would have certain basic spiritual experiences, we must have a clear understanding that the focus of God's economy is the mingled spirit, the divine Spirit mingled with the human spirit.

Those who live according to the flesh and the lusts of the flesh are the lowest type of people. Those who live according to the mind and the will are somewhat higher. Humanly speaking, those who live according to the conscience, which is part of man's spirit, may be considered the highest type of people. But we are even higher than this, for we live not only according to the conscience but according to the mingled spirit. Therefore, we are on the highest level. Here, on this level, we have the Christian life and also the church life. This is the focus of God's economy. We should walk according to this, that is, according to the mingled spirit. We should be a person in such a spirit as was the apostle John in Revelation (1:10). (*Basic Training,* pp. 55-56)

Further Reading: The Issue of the Union of the Consummated Spirit of the Triune God and the Regenerated Spirit of the Believers, chs. 2-3; *The Divine and Mystical Realm,* ch. 4; *Basic Training,* msg. 5

Enlightenment and inspiration: _____

_____

_____

_____

Morning Nourishment

Rom. That the righteous requirement of the law might be
8:4 fulfilled in us, who do not walk according to the flesh
    but according to the spirit.
Gal. But I say, Walk by the Spirit and you shall by no means
5:16 fulfill the lust of the flesh.

We all must realize that the most crucial part of our being is
our spirit....We have to learn to always live not in our flesh or in
our soul but in our spirit. When we are angry with someone, we
are often in our flesh. Then when we realize that we should be
nice to them, we act like gentlemen and talk very thoughtfully
with much logic. This is to talk, live, and behave ourselves in the
soul. Neither living in the flesh nor living in the soul count before
God. The book of 1 Corinthians reveals three kinds of persons: the
fleshly man, the soulish man, and the spiritual man. In 1 Corinthians 1—3 Paul condemns division because division is in the
flesh (1:10, 11; 3:3). Paul further tells us that we should not walk
in the soul (2:14). We should be neither fleshly men nor soulish
men. Rather, we should be spiritual, walking in our spirit
(2:11-13, 15). To be proper Christians, we must know that the
Lord Jesus today as the embodiment of the Triune God is the
Spirit (2 Cor. 3:17) indwelling our spirit and mingled with our
spirit as one spirit (1 Cor. 6:17).

God created us with a human spirit. Moreover, God is Spirit,
and He became incarnated, putting on flesh and blood. Then He
died, was buried, and in His resurrection He became the life-
giving Spirit. When we believed in Him, He entered into our spirit
as the life-giving Spirit. Now the Spirit works together with our
spirit, and the two spirits have become one to such an extent that
it is difficult to discern which is which. If we do not know our
spirit, we cannot live a proper Christian life. The Christian life is
altogether a life in our mingled spirit. (*Messages to the Trainees in
Fall 1990*, pp. 67-69)

Today's Reading

It is hard to tell if we are in the spirit. It is easier to know when we are not in the spirit. If we lose our temper, we know that is in the flesh. If we are so logical and philosophical, we know that is in the soul. When we are not in the spirit, we know it, but when we are in the spirit, we do not know it. This may be illustrated by the organs of our body. When there is no problem with our stomach, we are not aware of it, but when our stomach has a problem, we are aware of it....If we are certain that we know something in our spirit, this may indicate that we are not in the spirit.

In many verses in the New Testament, we cannot discern whether "spirit" denotes the divine Spirit or the human spirit. It simply denotes the wonderful mingled spirit in us....We have a spirit, and the divine Spirit mingles with our human spirit and is one spirit with our human spirit. We cannot analyze this; we can only believe it. We simply must do our duty to live, act, move, do things, and have our being in our spirit. (*Messages to the Trainees in Fall 1990,* pp. 69-70)

We need to see this vision. We need to see that the Triune God, the almighty God, who is Jehovah—the Father, the Son, and the Spirit, has become our all and has been wrought into us. Today He is in our spirit. The key to everything is found in this wonderful Spirit who is in our created and regenerated spirit and who has become one spirit with our spirit. This is the key and the starting point. If we do not turn to our spirit and pray out of our spirit, our prayers will be improper. If we do not enter into the mingled spirit and love others out of the mingled spirit, our love will be worthless. Anything that is not of the spirit is of the flesh and will not yield the fruit of the Holy Spirit. The Spirit of life will not confirm anything that is of the flesh.

Ultimately, the entire Bible requires only one thing of us—to walk according to the mingled spirit, which is the all-inclusive Spirit mingled with our regenerated spirit. (*Living in the Spirit,* pp. 26, 29)

Further Reading: Messages to the Trainees in Fall 1990, chs. 8-9; A Living of Mutual Abiding with the Lord in Spirit, chs. 4-5; The Practical Way to Live in the Mingling of God with Man, ch. 3

Enlightenment and inspiration: _____

_____

_____

_____

Morning Nourishment

Phil. ...Even now Christ will be magnified in my body....
1:20-21 For to me, to live is Christ...
    4:23 The grace of the Lord Jesus Christ be with your
         spirit.
    Gal. If we live by the Spirit, let us also walk by the Spirit.
    5:25

To live in the spirit is to let Christ fill and saturate us until He
permeates our whole being and is thereby expressed through us. It
is not a matter of husbands being able to love their wives or of wives
being able to love their husbands. Rather, it is a matter of living
in the spirit and allowing Christ as the life-giving Spirit to perme-
ate our entire being and to express God through us. This is the
overcoming life of a Christian, the family life of a Christian, and
the church life of a Christian. This is the reality of the church....
Today we need to forget about our thoughts, feelings, and everything else. We need to turn to our spirit and pay attention to being
in our spirit. Most people pay attention to their mind and their
feelings, but very few people pay attention to being in the spirit.
We all need to be absorbed with being in spirit. We may not know
what it is to bear the cross, but we should know what it is to follow
the spirit. We may not know what it means to pray and to fast, or
we may not know what it means to be humble and to be patient.
However, we should know how to follow the spirit. When we follow the spirit, we have humility and patience, and we spontaneously bear the cross. Once we follow the spirit, all things are ours.
(*Living in the Spirit*, p. 17)

Today's Reading

The highest teaching in the Scriptures is to live in the spirit....
Pursuing holiness, pursuing victory, bearing the cross, and receiv-
ing the discipline of the Holy Spirit are all matters in the Scriptures. However, these matters are all branches. The trunk, the
foundation, is living in the spirit....If we would live in the spirit,
pursuing patience and victory would be unnecessary. The reason
we need to be dealt with by the cross is because we live in the self.
However, if we would live in the spirit, there would be no need of

dealing when we encounter the cross. The dealing of the cross is for us to live in the spirit. When we endeavor to be dealt with by the cross apart from the spirit, we are merely changing our understanding of a situation. For example, perhaps a brother has wronged us, lied about us, or offended us. At first we may be unable to get over it, but later we may think, "Now I realize that the Lord is dealing with me in this way to break me. I am a stubborn old man, and no one can do anything about me. Therefore, God has given me such a brother....Now I understand that God is using that brother as an ax to break me. Therefore,...I would like to kiss the ax." We may have a change in understanding, but we still are not living in the spirit. We may endeavor to bear the cross three times in a day, but we still do not live in the spirit for even five minutes.

God needs a person who lives by Him. God does not need a person who lives by Him for five minutes and then stops....God needs people who will day and night, twenty-four hours a day, live in the spirit, live by Him, and live with Him as life.

The fact that we turn to the Lord only when the trials come proves that we do not live in the spirit. If we were to live in the spirit, it would not matter whether we were experiencing trials, temptations, favor, pity, or anything else. They would all be the same to us, because we would simply be living in the spirit. No matter what kind of wind would blow on us,...we would not be shaken. We would just live by our Lord and live in the spirit.

If we have seen the vision, we will see that the Lord's way today is to work Himself into us that we may live by Him. It is not a matter of living by Him in the mind but of living by Him in the spirit. If we would live by Him in this way day by day, our spirit would be living, flowing, and efficient. Moreover, we would be rich in experience and able to express those riches accordingly. In this way the church meetings will be delivered from ordinances....This way is the Lord's way, the proper way, for the preparation of His bride and for His coming back. (*Living in the Spirit,* pp. 37-39, 43)

Further Reading: Living in the Spirit, chs. 1-3; *Life Lessons,* lsn. 34

Enlightenment and inspiration: _____

_____

_____

_____

Morning Nourishment

1 Cor.	For even as the body is one and has many members,
12:12-13	yet all the members of the body, being many, are one body, so also is the Christ. For also in one Spirit we were all baptized into one Body, whether Jews or Greeks, whether slaves or free, and were all given to drink one Spirit.

Seeing the church is not the same as having the church. Rather, we must allow the element of God with man and man with God to be mingled in us and built up from us; only then will we have the reality of the church. The church is built upon the mingling of God with man and man with God. The church proceeds out of this mingling. The extent to which we are the church in reality depends upon how much this mingling has been built up in us....When we by the Lord's mercy allow the mingling of God with man and man with God to work and build in us, we will have the reality of the church.

The church is not a matter of name, position, or stand; neither is the church a matter of belief or organization. The church is a group of people who allow God to be mingled with them and who are mingled with God.

The principle of the Body is that our person is broken, defeated, and torn down by God and that we are giving God the opportunity to mingle with us and shine forth from within us. This is Christ being born again in the world; this is Christ being multiplied among us; this is the church, the enlargement of Christ. Whenever this is practiced, wherever this is present, there is the expression of the church on the earth—a church that is real, practical, actual, and powerful. Thus, the church with authority and image is a reality. (*The Church as the Body of Christ,* pp. 41, 46-47)

Today's Reading

The Body is a matter absolutely in the spirit, in our human spirit. Our regenerated spirit is indwelt by the Holy Spirit, but the emphasis with the Body of Christ today is on our human spirit rather than on the Holy Spirit. Therefore, in every chapter of the book of Ephesians there is something mentioned about our regenerated human spirit. Ephesians is a book on the Body, and every chapter contains a verse concerning the human spirit.

Ephesians 1 tells us that we can see the church only in our spirit (vv. 17-23). Ephesians 2 tells us that the building of the church, the Body, both universally and locally, is in our spirit (vv. 20-22). Then chapter three tells us that we need to be strengthened into our inner man, the regenerated human spirit (v. 16). Chapter four tells us that we are being renewed in the spirit of our mind (v. 23), and chapter five tells us that we need to be filled in our human spirit unto all the fullness of God (v. 18, with 3:19). Finally, chapter six tells us that we need to pray as the church, as the Body, in the spirit (v. 18). From all these verses we can see that the Body is altogether a matter in our spirit.

Whenever we turn to our spirit and exercise our spirit, we touch the Body, because the Body is in our spirit. When we exercise our spirit and touch the Body, not only do we have power, but we have the authority, because the Body is identified with the enthroned Head, with the lordship, with the headship, and with the kingship. The authority of the Head is with the Body. When you exercise your spirit, you touch the Body, and when you touch the Body, you are in the authority of the Head.

The power and the authority of the Head are in the Body,… and the Body is absolutely a matter in the spirit. Therefore, all the time we need to keep ourselves in our spirit connected to the Holy Spirit. Then we will have not only the power but also the authority of the Head. When we turn to the spirit, we get into the reality of the Body, and in the Body we are empowered and authorized by the Head. (*To Serve in the Human Spirit,* pp. 31, 49-51)

Further Reading: To Serve in the Human Spirit, chs. 3-4; *The Church as the Body of Christ,* chs. 3, 5; *The Issue of the Union of the Consummated Spirit of the Triune God and the Regenerated Spirit of the Believers,* ch. 1; *The Practical Points concerning Blending,* ch. 5; *Experiencing the Mingling of God with Man for the Oneness of the Body of Christ,* chs. 4-5*

Enlightenment and inspiration: _____

_____

_____

_____

Hymns, #1199

1   God's intention in this universe is with humanity,
So the Lord became the Spirit just with man to mingled be.
We rejoice that we can all partake of His economy.
    Yes, mingling is the way.

> Mingle, mingle, hallelujah,
> Mingle, mingle, hallelujah,
> Mingle, mingle, hallelujah,
> Yes, mingling is the way!

2   In the center of our being, past our mind, emotion, will,
Is a certain spot created to contain the Lord until
By His flowing and His flooding He will all our being fill;
    Yes, mingling is the way.

3   Now within the Lord's recov'ry, we're so glad to find the way
To experience the Triune God and live by Him today—
Get into the mingled spirit, and within the spirit stay;
    Yes, mingling is the way.

4   In the midst of seven lampstands, now the Son of Man
    we see;
Eyes ablaze and feet a'burning, He's for God's recovery.
God's intention He's accomplishing—a corporate entity;
    Yes, mingling is the way.

5   In our daily life and all we are and do and think and say,
How we need a deeper mingling just to gain the Lord
    each day;
Lord, we give ourselves completely just to take the
    mingled way.
    Yes, mingling is the way.

6   From the fruit of daily living, New Jerusalem we'll see,
It's the ultimate in mingling—it's divine humanity.
And what joy that we can share it all, and share it
    corporately.
    Yes, mingling is the way.

Composition for prophecy with main point and sub-points: _____

_____
_____
_____
_____
_____
_____
_____
_____
_____
_____
_____
_____
_____
_____
_____
_____
_____
_____
_____
_____
_____
_____
_____
_____
_____
_____
_____
_____
_____
_____
_____
_____
_____
_____
_____
_____
_____

Living in the Mingled Spirit
for the Reality of the Body of Christ
as Revealed in Romans

Scripture Reading: Rom. 1:9; 7:6; 8:4-6, 14, 16; 12:4-5; 16:16b

Day 1   I. **The book of Romans reveals the eight stages of the Christian life:**
   A. We were born sinful and under the righteous judgment of God (1:18—3:20).
   B. We have been justified through the redemption of Christ and regenerated by the Spirit (3:24; cf. 5:16).
   C. We realize that we were born in Adam and thus inherited sin and death (vv. 12-21).
   D. We have been baptized into Christ and are now in Christ (6:3).
   E. In Romans 7 we see a person striving and struggling in himself to do good, to keep the law of God, and to please God (vv. 18-19, 21-22).
   F. In Romans 8:1-17 we see one who walks according to the Spirit in the regenerated human spirit.
   G. The Lord arranges all things to work together for our conformation (vv. 28-30).
   H. According to the picture in Romans 12, the believers are living in the Body of Christ and are practicing the Body life.

Day 2 II. **In Romans we can see that God became man so that, in God's complete salvation, sinners may be redeemed, regenerated, sanctified, renewed, transformed, conformed, and glorified to become the sons of God, who are the same as God in life and nature, to be the members of the organic Body of Christ (8:3; 1:3-4; 3:24; 5:10; 8:14, 29-30; 12:2, 4-5).**

III. **The will of God is to obtain a Body for Christ to be His fullness, His expression (Rev. 4:11; Eph. 1:5, 9, 22-23; 5:17):**

A. According to Romans 12, the will of God is for us mutually to be members one of another, coordinating to be the Body of Christ and living the Body life (vv. 2, 4-5).

B. We coordinate and serve together in the Body of Christ for the building up of the Body of Christ in order to accomplish God's New Testament economy (vv. 6-11; Eph. 4:16; 1:10; 3:9; 1 Tim. 1:4).

Day 3   IV. **The focal point of the book of Romans is the Body of Christ (12:4-5):**

A. The Body is the channel on earth through which Christ continues His ministry from the heavens (Eph. 1:22-23).

B. If we neglect the Body of Christ, we do not have the focus of the Christian life, and we do not have the proper goal, aim, and direction in our Christian life.

C. Consecration is for the Body of Christ; the purpose of consecration is for us to realize the Body of Christ and to live the Body life (Rom. 12:1-2).

V. **The mingled spirit is the unique organ for God to bring forth and build up the Body of Christ (1:9; 7:6; 8:4, 14, 16; 12:4-5, 11):**

A. We must serve God in the regenerated spirit by the life-giving Spirit, not in the soul by the power and ability of the soul (1:9).

B. In order to reign in life for the Body life, we must be in the mingled spirit (5:17, 21).

C. The mingled spirit is a source of newness in our service to God (7:6).

D. The secret of God's organic salvation is the Spirit with our spirit (5:10; 8:16).

Day 4   E. The Body of Christ is an organism composed of a group of people who live, walk, and have their being according to the mingled spirit (vv. 4-6).

F. The mingled spirit is the spirit of sonship; if we are led by the Spirit in our spirit, we are sons of God in reality (vv. 14-15).

G. We need to pray in the mingled spirit (vv. 26-27).

H. In the mingled spirit we live a life of the highest virtues for the Body of Christ (12:9-21).

I. In the mingled spirit we live to the Lord and not to ourselves (14:7-9).

J. In the mingled spirit we live the kingdom life with righteousness, peace, and joy (v. 17).

K. When we live in the mingled spirit, we can be of the same mind, and with one accord and one mouth we can glorify God (15:5-6).

Day 5 **VI. Because Romans 12 is concerned with the function of the Body of Christ, it speaks of the Body from the angle of the organic union (vv. 4-5):**

A. If we do not see the organic union that we have with Christ, we cannot understand what the Body of Christ is (1 Cor. 1:30; 12:12-13, 27).

B. In order to be in the reality of the Body of Christ, we need to fully experience the organic union in Christ, with a thorough realization that we are organically one with Christ in life.

C. As we remain in the organic union, abiding in Christ as branches in the vine, we are actually living in the Body of Christ (John 15:1, 4-5).

D. The living of the Body life in the organic union with Christ involves our entire tripartite being (Rom. 12:1-2, 11):

1. We need to present our body a living sacrifice to God (v. 1).

2. We have to be renewed in the mind for the transformation of our soul (vv. 2-3).

3. We need to be burning in spirit with God as the fire (v. 11; Heb. 12:29).

E. If we do not live in the organic union and if we do not have our body offered, our soul transformed by the renewing of the mind, and our spirit burning, then, in a practical sense, we are outside of the Body and apart from the Body.

Day 6 **VII. The Body of Christ is unique in the universe, but it needs to be expressed on earth (Rom. 12:4-5; 16:16b; 1 Cor. 1:2; 12:12-13, 27; Col. 3:15; 4:15-16):**

A. The local churches are the expressions of the Body of Christ (Rom. 16:16b).

B. The Body of Christ and the local churches are two sides of one entity; the local churches are the Body of Christ, and the Body of Christ is the local churches.

C. The Body of Christ is the organism of the Triune God, and the local churches are for the fellowship and communication of the Body of Christ (vv. 1-23).

D. The local churches are the gathering point of our enjoyment of God's salvation in life (5:10; 16:16b).

E. As we enjoy God's life in the church life, we are saved from our self-view and self-goal and we care for the building up of Body of Christ (12:3; 14:7-9, 17-19; 15:1-3).

Morning Nourishment

Rom. That the righteous requirement of the law might
8:4 be fulfilled in us, who do not walk according to the
     flesh but according to the spirit.
   9 But you are not in the flesh, but in the spirit, if
     indeed the Spirit of God dwells in you....
  16 The Spirit Himself witnesses with our spirit that
     we are children of God.

In Romans 8 we see one who walks according to the Spirit in
his human spirit. However, many Christians do not know the difference between doing good and walking according to the Spirit.
Doing good is one thing; walking in the Spirit is entirely
another....We must be delivered from doing good to walking
according to the Spirit....One day the Lord opened my eyes to
show me that there was no need for me to try to do good....I was
in Christ,...the Holy Spirit was within me, and...consequently all
I had to do was simply follow the Spirit....After I saw this,...I
began to pray, "Praise You, Lord! Not only am I in You; Your Spirit
is within me. There is nothing for me to do or to try to do. All I
must do is simply enjoy and experience You. Hallelujah!" (*The
Practical Way to Live in the Mingling of God with Man*, pp. 11-12)

Today's Reading

[Romans 12] shows us one who is saved, walks according to
the Spirit, is being conformed to the image of Christ, and is a
member of the Body of Christ living in the Body of Christ and
practicing the Body life. Such a one realizes that he is not an individual person but a member of the Body.

In this stage, we can see the daily Christian living, which is a
living that is in the Body of Christ. Whatever we as Christians do,
we must do as members of the Body of Christ. In this stage, we
realize that we are no more independent and individual persons;
we are but members of the Body of Christ. From the time we have
this realization onward, we can never be independent or individualistic, because we are members of the Body. It is impossible for a
member of my physical body to be independent. If a member of

my physical body is independent, it is separate from the body and dies. Not only so, it becomes something that is dreadful and awful....Today many believers are like separated members of a human body—they are not only dead; they are dreadful. This is because they are separated from the Body of Christ. The more we live as members in the Body of Christ, the more dear and beloved we are to the other members. Hence, in the last stage of the Christian life as seen in the book of Romans, we see the Body of Christ composed of all the saved ones who live in the Body mutually as members. This is the maturity of the Christian life.

[There are] eight stages of the Christian life as seen in the Epistle to the Romans. In the first stage, we see a sinful person who is under the condemnation of God. The second stage presents to us a saved person—one who has been justified through the redemption of Christ. In the third stage, we see a person who, as a saved one, realizes that originally he was born in Adam. According to the fourth stage, we see how such a person realizes the fact that he is in Christ. The fifth stage presents to us a person who is fooled and tempted to try to do good by himself. In the sixth stage this person comes to know and realize that there is nothing left for him to do but to walk according to the Spirit. According to the seventh stage, this person accepts all the environments and circumstances from the sovereign hand of God for him to be conformed to the image of Christ. In the eighth and final stage, he realizes that he is a member of the Body of Christ and as such will never be independent or individualistic but will rather live, walk, act, and work as a member in the Body of Christ. We are no longer sinners in the world; we are members in the Body of Christ. As such, we must enjoy and experience Christ and walk, live, act, and work in the Body of Christ as His many members. (*The Practical Way to Live in the Mingling of God with Man,* pp. 14-15)

Further Reading: The Practical Way to Live in the Mingling of
   God with Man, ch. 1; *Crystallization-study of the Complete*
   Salvation of God in Romans, msg. 3

Enlightenment and inspiration: _____

_____
_____
_____

Morning Nourishment

Rom. **And do not be fashioned according to this age, but**
12:2 **be transformed by the renewing of the mind that**
you may prove what the will of God is, that which
is good and well pleasing and perfect.

4-5 **For just as in one body we have many members,**
and all the members do not have the same func-
tion, so we who are many are one Body in Christ,
and individually members one of another.

The book of Romans…mainly reveals that the Spirit who transforms sinners into sons of God is the Spirit of life….Romans tells us how the Triune God, in His consummation as the Spirit of life, makes sinners the sons of God who become the living members of the Body of Christ. These members, who form the Body of Christ, have been regenerated and possess God's Divine life and God's divine nature. Every member is wrapped up with the divine Trinity, who is being wrought into their tripartite being. Thus, they are being transformed, renewed, and even conformed to the image of the firstborn Son of God. Even their mortal bodies are being supplied with the divine life (Rom. 8:11) to make them living members of Christ. (*God's New Testament Economy,* pp. 125-126)

Today's Reading

Romans 12:1-2 tells us to present our bodies a living sacrifice and to be transformed by the renewing of the mind "that you may prove what the will of God is, that which is good and well pleasing and perfect." This verse speaks of "the" will of God….In speaking of the will of God, many Christians wrongly apply this verse. Strictly speaking, this verse indicates that the will of God is to have the church life. If we mean business with the Lord, present ourselves bodily to Him, and are willing to be transformed in our soul—our mind, emotion, and will—we will realize what God's will is in this universe and on the earth. God's will is nothing less than to have the church, that is, to have a Body for His Son. When we see this, we will sacrifice everything for it, because we will realize that this is the unique will.

By reading the entire context of Romans 12 we can realize what "the" will...of God is. It is to have the Body life, the church. This is the will of God. Of course the will of God includes other things, but all the other matters are secondary. The primary item of God's will is the church. No matter how good we are or how many things we do, if we are not in the church, if we do not practice the church life and live for the church, we are not in the will of God. I say this with certainty; we will be outside of the will of God, even though we are doing something for God.

Although the things mentioned in chapters twelve through sixteen may be considered the "wills" of God, the Body life is the foremost item. Chapters fourteen and fifteen tell us how to receive others, how to care for others, and how to avoid stumbling others, but all these matters are secondary. They depend on our practice of the church life. The first item that is revealed in chapters twelve through sixteen is the church, the Body, and all of the following items are supplementary to this will. Therefore, to prove what the will of God is, is to practice the church life. If we are proper members of the Body, acting and functioning in the church life, then we will have everything else. We will be persons in the will of God. (*A General Sketch of the New Testament in the Light of Christ and the Church, Part 2: Romans through Philemon,* pp. 128-129)

Now we are qualified to understand the will of God (12:2b). According to Romans 12, the will of God is for the saints mutually to be members one of another, coordinating to be the Body of Christ and living the Body life in it (v. 5). Furthermore, we coordinate and serve together with the saints in the Body of Christ for the building up of the Body of Christ in order to accomplish God's New Testament economy (vv. 6-11). (*Salvation in Life in the Book of Romans,* p. 29)

Further Reading: God's New Testament Economy, ch. 11; A General Sketch of the New Testament in the Light of Christ and the Church, Part 2: Romans through Philemon, ch. 11; Salvation in Life in the Book of Romans, ch. 4

Enlightenment and inspiration: _____

_____
_____
_____

Morning Nourishment

Rom. **...We serve in newness of spirit and not in oldness of**
7:6 letter.
5:17 ...Much more those who receive the abundance of
grace and of the gift of righteousness will reign in
life through the One, Jesus Christ.
1:9 For God is my witness, whom I serve in my spirit...

The book of Romans has four stations. The first is the station
of justification, then sanctification, then the Body, and then the
churches....From this sketch, there is no argument that the real
focus of this book is the Body. It is not even the churches, but the
Body. The churches are simply the expressions of the Body. It is
altogether right to say that Romans is a sketch of the Christian
life, but most of the teachers of the Bible didn't see the focus of the
Christian life. The focus of the Christian life is not justification
nor sanctification but the Body. If you miss the Body, you don't
have the center of the Christian life; you don't have the goal; you
don't have the aim; you don't have any direction. For what are you
sanctified? You are sanctified so that you can practically be a
member of the Body. (*Perfecting Training*, p. 279)

Today's Reading

The Body is the focus, the center, of the Christian life. By His
mercy, the Lord has shown us this vision. It is in the Bible; it is in
Romans, but Christians have not seen it....The way to walk as a
believer must be firstly to live in the Body.

What is the goal of consecration? If you read Romans 12:1-5
carefully, you can see that the purpose of consecration is so that
you can realize the Body. Consecration is for the Body.

The Body life is the first item of the believer's walk. If you
would know how to walk as a believer in Christ, the first item is to
live the Body life. Romans talks about the Body life in a way to
show us that this Body is the focus of the Christian life. (*Perfecting
Training*, pp. 279-280)

We need to realize that Satan hates the high peak of the divine
revelation concerning the ultimate goal of God's economy. He

hates this one main point—that God became a man so that man may become God in life and in nature but not in the Godhead to produce the organic Body of Christ for the fulfillment of God's economy to close this age and to bring Christ back to set up His kingdom....Today where is the Body of Christ on this earth? Today who understands and ministers and practices the Body of Christ? This is altogether something new. God purposely in His incarnation became a man that man may become God in life and nature but not in the Godhead for the producing of the organic Body of Christ to fulfill God's economy to close this age and to bring Christ back with His kingdom.

Today we have to know our mingled spirit and to exercise our spirit. This mingled spirit is the unique organ for God to bring forth and build up the Body of Christ. (*Crystallization-study of the Epistle to the Romans,* p. 159)

God's complete salvation is in one spiritual, practical, and experiential union of the Spirit of life with our spirit, forming a mingled spirit....The two spirits are not only united to be a union; they are also mingled to be a mingled spirit.

Romans 8:16a says, "The Spirit Himself witnesses with our spirit." The Spirit of God today, the all-inclusive Spirit of the Triune God, dwells in our regenerated human spirit and works in our spirit. These two spirits are one; they live together, work together, and exist together as one mingled spirit....We reign in life by the mingled spirit.

God's complete salvation is for us to reign in life by the abundance of grace (God Himself as our all-sufficient supply for our organic salvation) and of the gift of righteousness (God's judicial redemption applied to us in a practical way). When we are all reigning in life, living under the ruling of the divine life, the issue is the real and practical Body life. (*Crystallization-study of the Complete Salvation of God in Romans,* pp. 25, 29, 37)

Further Reading: Perfecting Training, ch. 24; *Crystallization-study of the Epistle to the Romans,* msg. 15

Enlightenment and inspiration: _____

_____

_____

_____

Morning Nourishment

Rom. For as many as are led by the Spirit of God, these are
8:14-15 sons of God. For you have not received a spirit of slavery *bringing you* into fear again, but you have received a spirit of sonship in which we cry, Abba, Father!

14:17 For the kingdom of God is not eating and drinking, but righteousness and peace and joy in the Holy Spirit.

The human spirit of the believers is the believers' spirit regenerated and indwelt by the divine Spirit of life and mingled with the divine Spirit of life as one spirit. It is through such a human spirit that the people chosen by God participate in the dynamic salvation of God as their living in this age and their destiny in eternity....We all have to know these two spirits in the divine enlightenment that we may enter, by the Spirit of life in our regenerated spirit which is mingled with the Spirit of life, into the intrinsic essence of the dynamic salvation of God in Christ, which is the Triune God processed and consummated to be our eternal inheritance for our enjoyment. (*Crystallization-study of the Epistle to the Romans*, pp. 174-175)

Today's Reading

Romans 8:4 says that we need to walk according to the spirit. According to what spirit shall we walk? It is not just according to the Holy Spirit nor just according to the human spirit. But it is according to the mingled spirit.

Even in the matter of being led by the Spirit as mentioned in verse 14, it is a matter of the human spirit with the Holy Spirit. The Spirit would never lead you apart from your spirit. He leads you when He is mingled with your spirit. He can never lead you unless your spirit is mingled by Him and with Him. What a subjective thing this is! By this you can see that few Christians today actually understand the Spirit's leading because they don't know they have a spirit. Even the more, they don't know that the Holy Spirit today is one with their spirit....The leading Spirit today is not only in our spirit, but also mingled with our spirit. It is such a

mingled spirit who is leading us....The Leader is in our spirit
[and]...makes our spirit a partnership of His leading....This is to
be led by the Spirit in and through and with our spirit.

Then we would cry, "I'm a son of God!..." Then we would witness, and we would groan, and He would intercede within us.
When we are in such a groaning, in such an interceding, we are
really one spirit with Him....We have no interest other than His.
When we are in this kind of situation, the law of the Spirit of life
works, setting us free. At that time no doubt we are actually sons
of God, and we are members of Christ. Right away we are in the
Body life. Now you see that the Lord couldn't have the Body life
for centuries because there were no Christians who were in such
a kind of situation—walking according to spirit, setting the mind
on the spirit, putting to death every practice of the body, being led
all the time, crying, witnessing, and groaning. We must be such a
person in such a living. Right away we will be in the Body of
Christ in an actual way. (*Perfecting Training,* pp. 350-351)

We do have such a mingled spirit within us, and what we
should do now is to behave, to act, to live, to walk, and to have
our being according to this mingled spirit. If we walk according to
this mingled spirit, we will be a son of God in full, and as such a
son we will be a living member of Christ, living in the church life
which is the kingdom of God. This kingdom is mentioned in
Romans 14:17 and is not mainly of power or ruling or govern-
ment. The kingdom of God, which is today's church life, is of righteousness with ourselves, peace toward others, and joy with God
in the Holy Spirit.... The kingdom of God today in the church life
is not for ruling or for governing but is for living—a righteous
living, a peaceful living, and a joyful living. The church life as
the kingdom of God today is a kingdom of righteousness, peace,
and joy in the Holy Spirit. This is the Lord's recovery. (*God's New
Testament Economy,* p. 133)

*Further Reading: Crystallization-study of the Epistle to the
Romans,* msg. 16; *Perfecting Training,* chs. 30-31

Enlightenment and inspiration: _____

_____

_____

_____

Morning Nourishment

1 Cor. For even as the body is one and has many mem-
12:12 bers, yet all the members of the body, being many,
       are one body, so also is the Christ.
Rom.   Do not be slothful in zeal, *but* be burning in spirit,
12:11 serving the Lord.

Two words from Romans 12:5 indicate the organic union—"in Christ." "In Christ" is a matter of the organic union. "We, who are many, are one Body in Christ." Just this one little phrase tells us from which angle Romans 12 speaks of the Body. It speaks from the angle of the life union, from the angle of the organic union. How then could we get into Christ? We were not born in Christ; we were born in Adam, but by being reborn we have been transplanted into Christ. We were dead in Adam, and God took us out of Adam and transplanted us into Christ by rebirth. This little phrase "in Christ" has been used many times in the New Testament. Whenever you read "in Christ," you must remember this indicates the organic union with Christ. (*Perfecting Training*, p. 273)

Today's Reading

Why does Romans 12 talk about the function of the Body? Because it talks about the Body based upon the organic union we have in Christ. In this union with Christ there is life. Dentures may be put into my mouth, but there is no organic union. The denture will not function because there is no organic union. We have to see that Romans 12 talks about the Body of Christ from the angle of the organic union, from the uniting life, from a life that unites us together, not only with Christ, but also with all the other members of Christ. Today the Christians know the Bible too superficially! Many teachers talk about Romans 12, but hardly one would tell you that Romans 12 talks about the Body from the angle of the organic union.

If we could not see the organic union that we have with Christ, we could never understand what the Body is. The Body does not mean simply that you love me and I love you.

We all have to realize the Body of Christ is altogether a matter of life that keeps us in an organic union with Christ. When we remain in this organic union, we are in the Body. When we don't remain in this organic union, we are out of the Body. You need to check yourselves for one day to see how much time you remain in this organic union. You will have to admit that you do not remain very much in this organic union. Occasionally we get there, but quite often we get out of there, so we are not in the Body. The actuality of the Body is the remaining in the organic union with Christ. If we are going to be actually living in the Body life, we must remain in the organic union with Christ. In other words, we must be remaining in Christ. So John 15 charges us to abide in Him. To abide in Him simply means to remain in this organic union. When we remain in this organic union, we are actually living in the Body. If we do not remain in this organic union with Christ, we have left the Body.

The Body is not an organization nor a society. The Body is not just a bunch of Christians coming together. The Body is something that is held together by the organic union with Christ. When we remain in the organic union with Christ, we are just living in the Body. Otherwise, we leave the Body.

To practice this Body life, you must first have your body offered to God. After having your body offered to God, you must have your soul transformed. You must be transformed in your soul by the renewing of your mind....This is absolutely and thoroughly needed. Our body must be offered and consecrated; our soul must be transformed by the renewing of our mind. Then our spirit has to be burning, to be on fire. If this is your case, I have the full confidence you are now practically in the Body life. If you don't realize the organic union in Christ and you do not have your body offered, your soul transformed by the renewing of the mind, or your spirit burning, you are just outside of the Body and apart from the Body, practically speaking. (*Perfecting Training,* pp. 274-275, 284)

Further Reading: Perfecting Training, chs. 23, 26, 40, 44

Enlightenment and inspiration: _____

_____

_____

Morning Nourishment

Rom. **For if we, being enemies, were reconciled to God**
5:10 **through the death of His Son, much more we will
be saved in His life, having been reconciled.**

16:16 **...All the churches of Christ greet you.**

14:19 **So then let us pursue the things of peace and the
things for building up one another.**

15:3 **For Christ also did not please Himself, but as it is
written, "The reproaches of those who reproached
You fell upon Me."**

The Body of Christ is first mentioned in the New Testament
in Romans 12....The last five chapters in Romans begin...with the
Body of Christ and conclude...with the local churches for the fellowship and communication of the Body of Christ. Do not think
that the local churches are one distinct side, and the Body of Christ
is another distinct side. These two sides are one entity. They refer
to the same thing. The Body of Christ is unique in the universe, but
it needs an expression on the earth. These expressions on the earth
are the local churches. The local churches are the Body of Christ,
and the Body of Christ is the local churches....We must see that the
Body of Christ is the very organism of the Triune God, and the local
churches are the fellowship and the communication of the Body of
Christ. (*Crystallization-study of the Epistle to the Romans,* pp. 4-5)

Today's Reading

The Body of Christ is unique in the universe. In the whole universe there is only one Body. The church of God is also unique in
the universe. This unique church of God in the universe becomes
the churches in the various cities locally in all five continents
through the spread of His children over all the earth. Every
believer can only live in the practical church life in one local
church. If anyone is not happy with the church where he is, he
may move to meet in another church. After a while, he may move
to yet another place to find a church that will satisfy him. This
kind of moving is not according to the will of God. God wants the

believers to live the church life locally, practically, and without any opinion.

The subject of Romans 16 is the local churches. Romans 1 talks about the just having life and living by faith (v. 17). Chapter five talks about the believers' justification unto life. Though chapter sixteen seems to only contain many verses which are just greetings, the focus of this chapter is not the greetings. This chapter shows us through the greetings the condition of the local churches at the time of Paul. The greetings manifest the condition of the churches.

First, in the church in Cenchrea, there was a sister named Phoebe who was a deaconess in the church....Second, the churches of the nations existed severally in various localities. They were not all in one locality (v. 4). Third, the church in the house of Prisca and Aquila was the church in Rome (16:3, 5a). This shows us that the number of saints in the church in Rome was probably not that large. Fourth, the churches of Christ were the local churches existing severally in various localities (16:16b). Fifth, the church of which Gaius was the host probably refers to the church in Corinth, which met in Gaius' house. All these items show us the condition of the local churches at that time.

The local churches are the gathering point of our enjoyment of God's salvation in life. After a man is saved, he will always try to find a church. There is no saved person who does not want to find a church. This is a wonderful thing! Hence, the church is the gathering point where saints receive grace. It is the gathering point of grace. If you want to see God's grace, you have to go to the church. Hence, this is the destination of our enjoyment of God's salvation in life. The more we enjoy God's salvation in life, the more we love to go to the church meetings. This is the place where we enjoy God's salvation in life unceasingly. Finally, the result of the enjoyment of God's life is our being saved from self-view and self-goal. (*Salvation in Life in the Book of Romans,* pp. 51-52)

Further Reading: Salvation in Life in the Book of Romans, chs. 5, 8-9

Enlightenment and inspiration: _____

_____

_____

_____

What Miracle! What Mystery!

1   What miracle! What mystery!
     That God and man should blended be!
     God became man to make man God,
     Untraceable economy!
     From His good pleasure, heart's desire,
     His highest goal attained will be.

2   Flesh He became, the first God-man,
     His pleasure that I God may be:
     In life and nature I'm God's kind,
     Though Godhead's His exclusively.
     His attributes my virtues are;
     His glorious image shines through me.

3   No longer I alone that live,
     But God together lives with me.
     Built with the saints in the Triune God,
     His universal house we'll be,
     And His organic Body we
     For His expression corp'rately.

4   Jerusalem, the ultimate,
     Of visions the totality;
     The Triune God, tripartite man—
     A loving pair eternally—
     As man yet God they coinhere,
     A mutual dwelling place to be;
     God's glory in humanity
     Shines forth in splendor radiantly!

Composition for prophecy with main point and sub-points: _____

_____

_____

_____

_____

_____

_____

_____

_____

_____

_____

_____

_____

_____

_____

_____

_____

_____

_____

_____

_____

_____

_____

_____

_____

_____

_____

_____

_____

_____

_____

_____

_____

_____

_____

_____

_____

Living in the Mingled Spirit
for the Reality of the Body of Christ
as Revealed in 1 Corinthians

Scripture Reading: 1 Cor. 15:45b; 6:17; 2:9-12, 14-15; 10:3-4, 16-17; 12:12-13, 27

Day 1 **I. God's economy is to work Himself into His chosen and redeemed people in order to make Himself one with them and to make them one with Him (Eph. 3:9, 14-19):**

A. In His economy God mingles Himself with His people to become one entity with them (4:4-6).

B. Concerning this oneness and mingling, 1 Corinthians 6:17 says that we who are joined to the Lord are one spirit; the divine Spirit and the human spirit have been mingled together to be one spirit.

C. The highest gospel is that we would be saved to the extent that God and we, we and God, are completely mingled as one, having one life and one living (1 John 4:15; John 15:4-5; Gal. 2:20; Phil. 1:19-21).

Day 2 **II. The expression *one spirit* in 1 Corinthians 6:17 indicates the mingling of the Lord as the Spirit with our spirit:**

A. The spirit, which is the mingling of our spirit and the Lord's Spirit into one spirit, is both the Spirit of the Lord and our spirit (Rom. 8:4; 2 Cor. 3:17; 1 Cor. 15:45b; 6:17).

B. All our spiritual experiences, such as our fellowship with the Lord, our prayer to Him, and our living with Him, are in this mingled spirit (1:9).

C. The implications of 1 Corinthians 6:17 are marvelous and far-reaching:

1. To be one spirit with the Lord implies that we are in Him and that He is in us (John 15:4-5).

    2. He and we have been mingled organically to become one in life (Rom. 8:10; Col. 3:4).

    3. First Corinthians 6:17 reveals that we andChrist are one wonderful, living entity (12:12).

    4. We, the complete and entire person, and the Lord are one spirit (6:17-20).

Day 3 **III. The mystery and depths of 1 Corinthians are the two spirits—the divine Spirit and the human spirit (12:13; 4:21):**

    A. God has revealed the hidden things by means of the two spirits (2:9-12).

    B. These two spirits are for our eating and drinking of the Lord; we eat the Lord and drink the Spirit in our spirit (10:3-4).

    C. God requires us to turn to our spirit so that we may be spiritual persons, who live and walk in the mingled spirit (2:14-15).

  IV. By being one spirit with the Lord, we can experience and enjoy Him as the all-inclusive One (1:2, 24, 30; 2:8, 10; 3:11; 5:7-8; 10:3-4; 11:3; 12:12; 15:20, 47, 45):

    A. When we are one spirit with the Lord, we enjoy the fellowship of God's Son, Jesus Christ our Lord (1:9).

    B. For anyone who is one spirit with the Lord, the supply is inexhaustible (15:10).

    C. The spirit of faith (2 Cor. 4:13) is the Holy Spirit mingled with our human spirit; we should exercise such a spirit to believe and to speak the things that we have experienced of the Lord.

Day 4 **V. First Corinthians 7 conveys the spirit of a person who loves the Lord, who cares for the Lord's interests on earth, who is absolutely for the Lord and one with the Lord, and who in every respect is obedient, submissive, and satisfied with God and the circumstances arranged by Him:**

    A. Paul had a spirit that was submissive, content,

and satisfied; in his spirit he was submissive to the Lord and content with his situation (vv. 17-24).

B. Because Paul was one with the Lord, when he spoke, the Lord spoke with him; thus, in 1 Corinthians 7 we have an example of the New Testament principle of incarnation (vv. 10, 12, 25, 40):

1. The principle of incarnation is that God enters into man and mingles Himself with man to make man one with Himself (1 John 4:15).

2. In the New Testament the Lord becomes one with His apostles, and they become one with Him and speak together with Him (1 Cor. 6:17).

3. In 7:25 and 40 we see the highest spirituality—the spirituality of a person who is so one with the Lord and permeated with Him that even his opinion expresses the Lord's mind.

Day 5 **VI. Through baptism and by drinking we are mingled with the Spirit (12:13):**

A. To be baptized in the Spirit is the initiation of the mingling and is once for all.

B. To drink the Spirit is the continuation of the mingling and is perpetual.

Day 6 **VII. The church as the Body of Christ is the corporate Christ, the Body-Christ (v. 12):**

A. The Body-Christ is composed of Christ Himself as the Head and the church as His Body with all the believers as His members.

B. Christ is both the Head and the Body (Eph. 4:15-16; 1 Cor. 12:12):

1. Christ in Himself is the Head, but when Christ is constituted into us, He is the Body (Col. 1:18a; 3:4, 10-11; 2:19).

2. Because Christ is both the Head and the Body, He is not only the individual Christ but also the Body-Christ.

C. The bread on the Lord's table signifies both the physical body of Jesus and the mystical Body of Christ, the corporate Christ, the Body-Christ (1 Cor. 10:16-17).

D. The Body-Christ is the issue of the full enjoyment of the riches of Christ (1:2, 30; 5:7-8; 10:3-4, 17; 12:12-13).

VIII. **The corporate Christ, the mystical Body of Christ, is the means for God to carry out His administration (Eph. 1:22-23; 1 Cor. 12:12-13, 27):**

A. The Body of Christ is for the Lord's move on earth (Eph. 4:16).

B. The Head is now carrying out God's administration through the Body (Rev. 5:6; Eph. 1:22-23; Rom. 12:4-5; Col. 1:18a; 2:19; 3:15; 1 Cor. 12:12-13, 27).

Morning Nourishment

1 John 4:15	Whoever confesses that Jesus is the Son of God, God abides in him and he in God.
John 15:4-5	Abide in Me and I in you. As the branch cannot bear fruit of itself unless it abides in the vine, so neither *can* you unless you abide in Me. I am the vine; you are the branches. He who abides in Me and I in him, he bears much fruit; for apart from Me you can do nothing.

God intends to work Himself into man to be man's life and life supply. Moreover, He wants to be altogether one with man. Because He desires to enter into us and to put us into Himself, we should abide in Him, and then He will also abide in us. Not only so, He and we, we and He, will live together. He will come into us to abide with us. He also wants us to live by Him and with Him. (*Living in the Spirit*, p. 32)

Today's Reading

The highest gospel is not merely concerning the forgiveness of sins and deliverance from hell that we may receive eternal blessing. Rather, the highest gospel is that we would be saved to the extent that God and we, we and God, are completely mingled as one, having one life and one living. We were fallen sinners—wicked, degraded, evil, and desolate—yet we can have one life and one living with God. God can abide with us and live with us....If we do believe this, it may be our belief in theory but not be our living. We may have been Christians for decades, yet we may have never had the deep realization that the gospel of God saves us into Him to live with Him so that He and we can have one life and one living....John 15:4...says, "Abide in Me and I in you."...John 6:57...says, "As the living Father has sent Me and I live because of the Father, so he who eats Me, he also shall live because of Me." These words are much deeper, showing us that the Lord is not only near us but is also mingled with us.

Today everything hinges on the fact that the Triune God as the all-inclusive Spirit is in our spirit to be our life and our all. We live by Him, and He and we are one—one in life and one in living. He is us, and we are Him.

We, however, have been so confused and mixed up because we have accumulated so many things within, such as human culture, religious concepts, ethical thoughts, and Christian doctrines.... We need to read the New Testament again. If we would read it in an unbiased way, we would bow our heads and say, "The fundamental thought, the central point, and the emphasis of the Bible is that God has become the life-giving Spirit, the all-inclusive Spirit." He has accomplished everything. He is waiting for us to receive Him into us. We all have a spirit to receive Him, and we all can live by Him. This is not a doctrine, an exhortation, or a religious regulation. Rather, this is a living Spirit, a living person, living in us, and we are living by Him. Everything is here. If we have this, we have everything. (*Living in the Spirit,* pp. 32, 41)

First Corinthians 15:45b tells us that the last Adam, the Lord Jesus our Savior, became a life-giving Spirit. This Spirit has also come into our spirit. Therefore, 1 Corinthians 6:17 says that we have become one spirit with the Lord. Within us there truly is the fact that the two spirits are mingled as one spirit.

The highest Christian life is a life of the two spirits becoming one spirit. This surpasses ethics and morality. Today you and I do not merely have a conscience, the innate knowledge of good and the innate ability to do good, or the bright virtue, nor do we only have a created spirit. Within our created spirit we also have the Spirit of God, who is our Redeemer and who became the life-giving Spirit. Today I want to help everyone to practice living by this mingled spirit, that is, to practice being one spirit with the Lord. Your being saved is not just a matter of your sins being forgiven, your being cleansed by the blood, or your being redeemed and regenerated. More than that, the Lord as the Spirit has entered your regenerated spirit and mingled with your regenerated spirit to become one spirit. This is the most precious point. (*A Living of Mutual Abiding with the Lord in Spirit,* p. 64)

Further Reading: Living in the Spirit, chs. 2-3

Enlightenment and inspiration: _____

_____

_____

_____

Morning Nourishment

1 Cor. But he who is joined to the Lord is one spirit....Or do
6:17, you not know that your body is a temple of the Holy
19-20 Spirit within you, whom you have from God, and
you are not your own? For you have been bought
with a price. So then glorify God in your body.

In 1 Corinthians 6:17 Paul says, "He who is joined to the Lord is one spirit." In this verse the word "joined" refers to the believers' organic union with the Lord through believing into Him (John 3:15-16). This union is a matter not only of the divine life but in the divine life. The organic union with the resurrected Lord can only be in our spirit.

The words "one spirit" indicate the mingling of the Lord as the Spirit with our spirit. Our spirit has been regenerated by the Spirit of God (John 3:6), who is now in us (1 Cor. 6:19) and who is one with our spirit. Through resurrection the Lord became the life-giving Spirit, and as such a Spirit He is now with our spirit (2 Tim. 4:22). Hence, the one spirit in 1 Corinthians 6:17 is the mingled spirit, our regenerated human spirit mingled with the divine Spirit.

Every regenerated person has two spirits within him. First, a regenerated person has a regenerated human spirit. Second, dwelling within the regenerated human spirit there is the Spirit of God. (*The Divine Dispensing of the Divine Trinity,* p. 291)

Today's Reading

Since we are joined to the Lord, we are one spirit with the Lord. This means that the spirit, which is the mingling of our spirit and the Lord's Spirit into one spirit, is both the Spirit of the Lord and our spirit; it is the Lord's Spirit mingled with our spirit and our spirit mingled with the Lord's Spirit. The New Testament, in verses such as Romans 8:4-6 and Galatians 5:16 and 25, often uses this word, the spirit, which is the mingled spirit, to speak concerning what the Lord is to us and concerning our experience of the Lord. All our spiritual experiences after we are saved, such as our fellowship with the Lord, our prayer to

Him, our living with Him, and our obedience to Him, are in this spirit, the Lord's Spirit and our spirit mingled into one. (*Life Lessons,* vol. 3, p. 45)

First Corinthians 6:17…is a strong word. Paul did not merely say that the Spirit mingles with our spirit or that these two spirits become one spirit. He said that we, the complete and entire person, and the Lord are one spirit. We have stressed very much that the Spirit indwells our spirit. Although this is correct, we need to see something further. First Corinthians 3:16 says that we are the temple of God and the Spirit of God dwells in us, the whole persons. We are composed of spirit, soul, and body. Since we are the temple of God, the Spirit is in our body, our soul, and our spirit. To say that the Spirit is in our spirit is correct. However, to say that the Spirit is only in our spirit and not in our body or mind is not right in every sense. The Spirit is not only in our spirit but also in our body. First Corinthians 6:13-20 speaks of the sanctification of the body. The subject of this portion of the Word is the body. In this section Paul says, "Or do you not know that your body is a temple of the Holy Spirit within you, whom you have from God, and you are not your own?" (v. 19). Our body is the temple of the Holy Spirit.

The Bible goes so far as to say that our entire being is one spirit with the Lord. Our faith has to go this far also. Whether or not we believe this, God considers it to be so. As long as one is a believer in Christ, he as a person and the Lord our Savior as a person are one spirit. Not only are our spirit and soul the temple of the Holy Spirit, but also our body is His temple. The more we believe this, the more we will experience it.…We all have to believe that there is a divine Spirit and a human spirit, and because there are these two spirits, God and we, we and God, can be one spirit. We should go so far as to say not only that the divine Spirit is in our spirit but also that we ourselves and God are one spirit. (*Messages to the Trainees in Fall 1990,* pp. 62-63)

Further Reading: The Divine Dispensing of the Divine Trinity, chs. 28, 30; *Messages to the Trainees in Fall 1990,* ch. 8; *Life Lessons,* lsn. 30

Enlightenment and inspiration: _____

_____

_____

_____

Morning Nourishment

1 Cor. God is faithful, through whom you were called into
1:9 the fellowship of His Son, Jesus Christ our Lord.
10:3-4 And all ate the same spiritual food, and all drank the
same spiritual drink; for they drank of a spiritual
rock which followed *them*, and the rock was Christ.
12:3 Therefore I make known to you that no one speaking
in the Spirit of God says, Jesus *is* accursed; and no
one can say, Jesus *is* Lord! except in the Holy Spirit.

We need to feed on Jesus every day. By so doing, we will grow, and by growing, we will be transformed. This will cause us to become a solid piece of precious material that is good for the building up of the church.

This is the reason that for many centuries the subtle enemy, Satan, has hidden the matter of eating and drinking the Lord from God's children. We praise the Lord that in these last days the Lord is recovering this matter. He is removing the veils of religion, our old background, our old doctrines, and our old concepts that we may know His economy. His way to dispense Himself into us is not by teaching but by our eating and drinking the Lord Jesus.... The mystery and depths of 1 Corinthians are the two spirits, the divine Spirit and the human spirit. These two spirits are for our eating and drinking the Lord. We eat the Lord and drink the divine Spirit in our human spirit. Therefore, we all need to apply our human spirit by calling on the name of the Lord Jesus. To call on the Lord is to eat and drink of Him. This is the strategic point in 1 Corinthians. (*The Enjoyment of Christ for the Body in 1 Corinthians*, pp. 24-25)

Today's Reading

One who lives in the mingled spirit is a spiritual man. A spiritual man stands in contrast to the soulish man. According to the context of these chapters, to be soulish is...to live according to Greek culture. Philosophers and those who admire human wisdom are soulish people. The spiritual persons are those who exercise their spirit to coordinate with the Spirit of God. Because they live in the mingled spirit, they are truly spiritual and they have spiritual knowledge, discernment, and communication. Here in the mingled spirit we enjoy Christ not in a superficial way, but as the depths of God and even in the depths of God. We enjoy Him in a way that eye has not seen, ear has not heard, mind has not thought, and heart has never imagined. We enjoy Christ in a way beyond all we have ever dreamed.

God has predestined Christ for us, He has prepared Him for us, He has revealed Him to us, and He has given Him to us as the deep things of God. How wonderful! We need to pray more concerning these matters, especially that we shall see this vision clearly. We also need to practice the mingled spirit in order to be spiritual. Then we shall be able to discern the things of man and of God and to communicate with others spiritually in the mingled spirit....If we experience the mingled spirit in this way, we shall have the deeper experience of Christ. We shall experience Him not in a superficial way, but as the depths of God....Praise the Lord that He is our portion through the mingled spirit! (*Life-study of 1 Corinthians,* p. 165)

Day by day we all need to call, "O Lord Jesus." When we call on this dear name, we receive His precious person as the life-giving Spirit. Then He becomes whatever we need. If we need righteousness, He is our righteousness. If we need sanctification, He is our sanctification....Whenever we say, "Lord Jesus!" we are in the Spirit, and we are drinking the one Spirit. By drinking the Spirit, we become one spirit with the Lord Jesus (6:17). He is the life-giving Spirit, and we have all been put into Him and have been positioned to drink of Him day by day....We are in the Spirit, and we are drinking the Spirit. As a result, the Spirit is in us, and we are one spirit with the Lord. In this one spirit we experience Christ as our light, life, power, holiness, sanctification, and everything. In this spirit we also have the church life. (*The Enjoyment of Christ for the Body in 1 Corinthians,* pp. 14, 16)

Further Reading: The Enjoyment of Christ for the Body in 1 Corinthians, chs. 1-2; *Life-study of 1 Corinthians,* msg. 18

Enlightenment and inspiration: _____
_____
_____
_____

Morning Nourishment

1 Cor. But to the married I charge, not I but the Lord...
7:10, 12 But to the rest I say, I, not the Lord...
   25 Now concerning virgins I have no commandment
      of the Lord, but I give *my* opinion as one who has
      been shown mercy by the Lord to be faithful.
   40 But she is more blessed if she so remains, accord-
      ing to my opinion; but I think that I also have the
      Spirit of God.

First Corinthians 7 is the writing of a man, yet this composition became the divine revelation. He could say that his word was not the commandment of the Lord, but the word he gave became the divine revelation....Paul concludes by saying that what he had given was according to his opinion and that he thought that he also had the Spirit of God. He not only had his opinion, but he also had the Spirit of God. These two things speak together in the mingled way: the Spirit of God speaks in his opinion, and his opinion expresses something with the Spirit of God. God mingled with man as one person with two natures, living together in one life and one living, is the experience of the grafted life in the principle of incarnation. This is the real dealing with the disposition. (*The Experience and Growth in Life*, pp. 171-172)

Today's Reading

When Paul wrote 1 Corinthians 6:17, he was full of assurance. He had the confidence that he was one spirit with the Lord....But in 7:40 he says, "I think that I also have the Spirit of God."

At the end of 1 Corinthians 7, a long chapter concerned with married life, Paul says, "I think that I also have the Spirit of God" (v. 40). In the previous chapter Paul said that he was one spirit with the Lord. But in 7:40 he says, "I think that I also have the Spirit of God." This indicates that he may not have been sure. I did not know how to reconcile these verses.

In 7:10 Paul says, "I charge, not I but the Lord." In verse 12 he says, "I say, I, not the Lord." In verse 25 he goes on to say, "I have no commandment of the Lord, but I give my opinion." Then in verse 40 he says, "But she is more blessed if she so remains, according to my opinion; but I think that I also have the Spirit of God." All these verses indicate the New Testament principle of incarnation—the principle of God and man, man and God, becoming one. This differs drastically from the principle of Old Testament prophecy—speaking for God. In the Old Testament the word of Jehovah came to a prophet (Jer. 1:2; Ezek. 1:3), the prophet being simply the mouthpiece of God. But in the New Testament the Lord becomes one with His apostles, and they become one with Him. As a result, both speak together. His word becomes their word, and what they utter is His word. Hence, the apostle's charge is the Lord's charge (1 Cor. 7:10). What he says, though not by the Lord, still becomes a part of the divine revelation in the New Testament (v. 12). He is so one with the Lord that even when he gives his own opinion, not the commandment of the Lord (v. 25), he still thinks that he also has the Spirit of God. He does not claim definitely to have the Spirit of God, but he *thinks* that he *also* has the Spirit of God. This is the highest spirituality, the spirituality based on the principle of incarnation. (*The Divine Dispensing of the Divine Trinity,* p. 274)

Here we see the…spirituality of a person who is so one with the Lord that even his opinion expresses the Lord's mind. Paul was absolutely one with the Lord and thoroughly saturated with Him. Because his entire being was permeated with the Lord, even his opinion expressed the mind of the Lord. For this reason, we say that verse 25 expresses the highest spirituality.

We need to see the principle of incarnation illustrated here and receive mercy and grace from the Lord to speak in a genuine and frank manner without any pretense. In order to speak like this we need to be saturated with the Spirit. Then what we utter or express will be our thought, our opinion, but it will also be something of the Lord because we are one with Him. (*Life-study of 1 Corinthians,* pp. 381-383)

Further Reading: The Experience and Growth in Life, msgs. 25, 29; *Life-study of 1 Corinthians,* msg. 43

Enlightenment and inspiration: _____

_____

_____

_____

Morning Nourishment

1 Cor. **But of Him you are in Christ Jesus, who became**
1:30   **wisdom to us from God: both righteousness and**
     sanctification and redemption.
12:13 **For also in one Spirit we were all baptized into one**
     Body, whether Jews or Greeks, whether slaves or
     free, and were all given to drink one Spirit.
15:45 **...The last Adam *became* a life-giving Spirit.**

[First Corinthians 12:13 speaks of the Spirit and the Body.] As the Spirit is the sphere and element of our spiritual baptism and in such a Spirit we were all baptized into one organic entity, the Body of Christ, so we should all, regardless of our races, nationalities, and social ranks, be this one Body. Christ is the life and constituent of this Body, and the Spirit is the reality of Christ. It is in this one Spirit that we were all baptized into this one living Body to express Christ.

The believers of Christ are baptized through water and in the Spirit into Christ, the death of Christ (Rom. 6:3), the name—the person—of the Triune God (Matt. 28:19), and the Body of Christ. Baptism ushers the believers into an organic union with Christ and the Triune God, making them living members of the Body of Christ. (*The Divine Dispensing of the Divine Trinity*, p. 320)

Today's Reading

To be baptized in the Spirit is to get into the Spirit and be lost in Him. To drink the Spirit is to take the Spirit in and have our being saturated with Him. By these two procedures we are mingled with the Spirit. To be baptized in the Spirit is the initiation of the mingling and is once for all. To drink the Spirit is the continuation and accomplishment of the mingling and is perpetual, forever. (*The Divine Dispensing of the Divine Trinity*, p. 321)

According to 1 Corinthians 1:30, we believers are all in Christ, and according to 15:45, Christ is the life-giving Spirit. Therefore, we are in the Spirit. This indicates that we have all been baptized in the Spirit. This is truly scriptural and logical. From now on, if anyone asks if we have been baptized in the Spirit, we should say,

"I am in Christ. Therefore, I am in the life-giving Spirit." In Greek, *were all baptized* in 12:13 is in the aorist tense, indicating that our baptism in the Spirit has been accomplished. We have all been baptized in one Spirit.

To be baptized is to be put into water, but to drink is to take the water into us. Many in Christianity pay attention to baptism, but they neglect drinking. Our baptism in the Spirit has been accomplished, but our drinking the Spirit is ongoing. Through baptism we have been positioned to drink the Spirit; therefore, now we need to drink all day long.

We should not count on our feelings as proof that we have been baptized in the Spirit. Our feelings can be very deceptive. After speaking for an entire chapter concerning marriage life, Paul said, "I think that I also have the Spirit of God" (7:40). It seems that he did not have much assurance....Because Paul was a person who lived in the mingled spirit,...whatever he said was God's word, even though he did not have a strong feeling about it. This illustrates that we should not care for our feelings. We must care only for the facts and the practicality. The fact is that we were all baptized into Christ, who is the life-giving Spirit. When we believed in Him and called on His name, we entered into Him, and He entered into us. Now we all need to take this fact and call on His name hour after hour. We may compare calling to breathing. We are in the air around us, but by our breathing, the air enters into us. On the one hand, we are in the air, and on the other hand, the air is in us. Eventually, we become one with the air. Likewise, our breathing the Lord Jesus as the life-giving Spirit makes us one spirit with Him. By our breathing and drinking the one Spirit, He comes into us more and more. As a result, whatever we do and say is something of the Lord....This kind of experience is the proper Christian life that issues in the church life. (*The Enjoyment of Christ for the Body in 1 Corinthians*, pp. 15-17)

Further Reading: The Divine Dispensing of the Divine Trinity, chs. 33-34; *Life-study of 1 Corinthians,* msgs. 52, 58

Enlightenment and inspiration: _____

_____

_____

_____

Morning Nourishment

1 Cor. **Seeing that there is one bread, we who are many**
10:17   **are one Body; for we all partake of the one bread.**
12:12   **For even as the body is one and has many mem-**
        bers, yet all the members of the body, being many,
        are one body, so also is the Christ.
Col.   **...Holding the Head, out from whom all the Body...**
2:19   **grows with the growth of God.**

Most Christians realize that Christ is the Head, but they do not consider that He is also the Body....We consider that Christ is the Head and that the church is the Body. Strictly speaking, however, this is a wrong concept. It is wrong to say that a man's head is the man himself but that his body is someone else. A man is a whole person, including his head and his body. Likewise, Christ is a complete person, both the Head and the Body.

Since Christ is both the Head and the Body, He is the Body-Christ....He is no longer only the individual Christ; He is also the corporate Christ....Individually, He is Christ, and corporately, He is the Body-Christ. (*The Enjoyment of Christ for the Body in 1 Corinthians,* pp. 30-31)

Today's Reading

On the Lord's table there are the bread and the cup. The bread signifies Christ's body in two aspects. First, it signifies the physical body of Jesus...and second, it signifies the mystical Body of Christ. The mystical Body of Christ is the corporate Christ, the Body-Christ. When we partake of the bread at the Lord's table, we are eating not only the individual Christ but also the corporate Christ,...the mystical Body of Christ.

First Corinthians tells us that we need to enjoy and partake of all the riches of Christ by calling, "O Lord Jesus." In this way He becomes our power, wisdom, righteousness, sanctification, redemption, the deep things of God, the foundation, the Passover, our spiritual food, spiritual drink, and spiritual rock, the Head, the firstfruits, the second man, the last Adam, the life-giving Spirit, the Body, and the Body-Christ. The issue of this enjoyment

of Christ is the church life....The Body comes out of the enjoyment of Christ. By our calling on this rich Christ, on the Lord who
is rich to all, He enters into us, and we digest and assimilate Him
so that He comes into every part of our being to be our organic element, even to become us.

As human beings who have eaten, digested, and assimilated
the Triune God, we now have the divine element. Moreover, since
we have the divine element in a corporate way, we are the
Body-Christ. The proper church life, the Body-Christ, comes out
of our eating the Triune God. This is a wonderful and marvelous
matter. This is God's intention, desire, and eternal purpose (Eph.
3:9-11). How subtle the enemy of God is! The old serpent has crept
in deceitfully to deaden the living of the believers and cause divisions through differing teachings and opinions. This is why in
today's Christianity we do not see the Body-Christ, the corporate
Jesus. Instead, what we see are many divisions. (*The Enjoyment
of Christ for the Body in 1 Corinthians,* pp. 31, 38)

The Body is an organism for Christ as the believers' life to
grow and express Himself. The church is an assembly for God
to operate His administration. Therefore, in chapter twelve in
dealing with the gifts, four matters are emphasized: speaking,
the Spirit, the Body, and administration. Speaking ushers us
into the Spirit, the Spirit brings us into the Body, and the Body
keeps us in the Spirit....If this is our situation, the Body is not
divided; rather, it remains one in the Spirit. Then the Body is
qualified for the carrying out of God's administration. The Body in
the sense of being the church is the means for God to adminis-
trate on earth....Thus, we go from speaking, to the Spirit, to the
Body, and, ultimately, to God's administration. The Lord's coming
back will be the ultimate consummation, the peak, of His administration. What we are doing in the Lord's recovery is preparing
the way to bring Him back. (*Life-study of 1 Corinthians,* pp. 532-533)

*Further Reading: The Enjoyment of Christ for the Body in 1 Corin-
thians,* chs. 3-4; *Life-study of 1 Corinthians,* msg. 59

Enlightenment and inspiration: _____

_____

_____

_____

Hymns, #745

1   O Lord, Thou art the Spirit now
Who in our spirit lives;
One spirit have the two become,
Which oneness to us gives.

2   Thy Spirit with our spirit, Lord,
The witness ever bears
That we the Father's children are
And of God's glory heirs.

3   'Tis in our spirit Thee we touch
Thy riches to enjoy,
And as the Spirit Thou dost give
Thyself without alloy.

4   'Tis in our spirit we may walk
And follow Thee alway,
While, as the Spirit, Thou dost lead
And light impart each day.

5   In spirit, by Thy Spirit, Lord,
We live and worship Thee;
Thou, in our spirit, thru Thine own
Strengtheneth constantly.

6   In spirit, with Thy Spirit, Lord,
We offer prayer to Thee,
While, as the Spirit, Thou in us
Groanest unutterably.

7   We to our spirit would return
And there would contact Thine;
'Tis in the spirit we may share
Our heritage divine.

8   What oneness, O my Lord, is this—
Two spirits intertwine!
Thy Spirit in our spirit lives,
And ours abides in Thine!

Composition for prophecy with main point and sub-points: _____

_____
_____
_____
_____
_____
_____
_____
_____
_____
_____
_____
_____
_____
_____
_____
_____
_____
_____
_____
_____
_____
_____
_____
_____
_____
_____
_____
_____
_____
_____
_____
_____
_____
_____

Living in the Mingled Spirit
for the Reality of the Body of Christ
as Revealed in Ephesians
(1)

Scripture Reading: Eph. 1:17-23; 4:3-4, 17-24

Day 1 I. **Paul's Epistle to the Ephesians reveals that we can live in the reality of the Body of Christ by living in the mingled spirit (Rom. 8:16; 1 Cor. 6:17; Eph. 1:17; 2:22; 3:5, 16; 4:23; 5:18; 6:18):**

A. The reality of the Body of Christ is the reality in Jesus, the actual condition of the God-man living of Jesus recorded in the four Gospels, duplicated in the many members of His Body to be the corporate God-man living of the one new man, a living by the Spirit of the glorified Jesus mingled with our spirit for us to keep the oneness of the Spirit with the transformed human virtues enriched by and with the divine attributes (4:17-24; John 7:37-39; Eph. 4:3-4).

B. The reality of the Body of Christ is the Spirit of reality, who is the reality of the processed Triune God, mingled with our spirit; when we live in the mingled spirit, we are learning Christ as the reality is in Jesus in order to have a corporate living of being conformed to the death of Christ by the power of His resurrection for His corporate expression (1 John 5:6; John 14:17; 16:13; Acts 16:7; Phil. 1:19-21a; 3:10; Gal. 6:17).

Day 2 II. **We must pray for a spirit of wisdom and revelation so that the eyes of our heart may be enlightened to see the mystery of God's economy, which is to dispense Christ as the mystery of God into God's chosen people to make them the reality of the Body of Christ as the mystery of Christ (Eph. 1:9, 17-18; 3:3-5, 9; 5:32; 6:19; Col. 2:2):**

A. The Body of Christ is not a doctrine but a realm; only a revelation from God in our spirit will usher us into the realm of the Body, and only then will the Body become our experience (Eph. 1:17-23; 3:14-19; cf. John 3:3, 5).

B. In order to receive the revelation of the great mystery of Christ and the reality of the Body of Christ, we must cooperate with the Lord to be poor in spirit and pure in heart (Eph. 1:17-18a; 3:16-17a; Matt. 5:3, 8; Isa. 57:15; 66:1-2; 1 Pet. 3:4).

Day 3

C. We need a spirit of wisdom and revelation to see and know Christ as the hope of God's calling (Eph. 1:17-18; 4:4b; cf. 2:12; 1 Cor. 15:19):

1. God's upward calling is for us to fully enjoy and gain the all-inclusive Christ in this age so that we may be rewarded with the uttermost enjoyment of Christ as our prize in the next age (Phil. 3:8, 14).

2. The hope of our calling, our living hope, our hope of glory, is the resurrected Christ Himself as the life-giving Spirit mingled with our spirit (1 Pet. 1:3; Col. 1:27; Rom. 5:2-5; 15:13).

3. Christ Himself as the eternal life in our spirit enables us to have a hope for this age, for the coming age, and for eternity (Titus 1:2):

   a. In this age we have the hope of growing in life, of maturing in life, of manifesting our gifts, of exercising our functions, of being transformed, of overcoming, of being redeemed in our body, and of entering into glory (Rom. 8:2, 4, 6, 11, 23-25; Phil. 3:21).

   b. In the coming age we have the hope of entering into the kingdom, of reigning with the Lord, and of enjoying the blessings of eternal life in the manifestation of the kingdom (Matt. 19:29; Rev. 5:10).

   c. In eternity we have the hope of being fully deified to become the New Jerusalem so that we may participate fully in the consummate enjoyment of Christ as the consummated blessings of the eternal life in its ultimate manifestation (1 John 3:2-3; Rev. 21:1-7; 22:1-2, 14).

Day 4 D. We need a spirit of wisdom and revelation to see and to know Christ as the riches of the glory of God's inheritance in the saints (Eph. 1:18b; Acts 26:18):

   1. We are being designated by God to be His inheritance for His enjoyment so that we may inherit God as our inheritance for our enjoyment (Eph. 1:18b, 14).

Day 5   2. We are being designated to be God's inheritance for His enjoyment by remaining in the finer dispensing of the sealing Spirit in our spirit so that we are inscribed with the Spirit of the living God as the divine element of God, causing us to bear the divine image of God to display His divine ownership of our entire being (v. 13; 4:30; 2 Cor. 3:3).

   3. We are inheriting God as our inheritance for our enjoyment by remaining in the fresh dispensing of the pledging Spirit in our spirit so that we are filled with the unsearchably rich Christ as a foretaste of what we will inherit of God in full at the redemption, the transfiguration, of our body (Eph. 1:14; 3:8; 2 Cor. 4:7; Rom. 8:23; Phil. 3:21).

Day 6 E. We need a spirit of wisdom and revelation to see and to know the transcending Christ as the surpassingly great power of the Triune God (Eph. 1:19-23) "toward us who believe" (v. 19) and "to the church" (v. 22):

   1. Christ as the Spirit of the resurrecting Triune God mingled with our spirit (Rom. 8:10-11) is our resurrecting power (Eph.

1:20a), ascending power (v. 20b), subjecting power (v. 22a), and heading-up power (v. 22b); this fourfold power is transmitted to the church, the Body of the Head (vv. 22-23a).

2. *Toward us who believe* and *to the church* indicate that the divine power, which includes all that the Triune God has passed through, has been installed into us once for all and is being transmitted into us continually, causing us to enjoy Christ richly and to have the proper church life.

3. Since the transcending Christ is the embodiment of the Triune God, His transcending transmission includes all the rich dispensing of the Triune God; when the riches of Christ are assimilated into our being metabolically, they constitute us to be the fullness of Christ, the Body of Christ, as His expression (vv. 22-23; 3:8).

4. In order to participate in the transmitting of Christ as the resurrecting, ascending, subjecting, and heading-up power to the church, we must know, use, and exercise our spirit; because Christ as the power of God (1 Cor. 1:24) dwells in our spirit, our spirit is a spirit of power (2 Tim. 1:7); by exercising our spirit, we are able to do all things in Christ, and He is able to do all things in us as the empowering One (Phil. 4:13; 3:21) to transform us from glory to glory (2 Cor. 3:18) for His glory in the church (Eph. 3:20-21).

Morning Nourishment

Eph. If indeed you have heard Him and have been taught
4:21 in Him as the reality is in Jesus.
John *Even* the Spirit of reality, whom the world cannot
14:17 receive, because it does not behold Him or know
Him; but you know Him, because He abides with you
and shall be in you.
Acts ...When they had come to Mysia, they tried to go into
16:7 Bithynia, yet the Spirit of Jesus did not allow them.

The reality in Jesus is the real situation of the life of Jesus as
recorded in the four Gospels....Jesus lived a life always doing
things in God, with God, and for God. God was in His life, and He
was one with God. This is the reality in Jesus. We, the believers,
regenerated with Christ as our life and taught in Him, learn from
Him as the reality is in Jesus.

In His thirty-three and a half years on earth, the Lord Jesus
formed the mold, the pattern, to which all those who believe in Him
are to be conformed. According to the record of the four Gospels,
the life of the Lord Jesus was a life of reality....That life of reality
was the very expression of God. For this reason Paul says that we
learn Christ as the truth is in Jesus. In other words, we learn
Christ according to the mold of the life of Jesus. The mold of the
life of Jesus is the reality. (*Life-study of Ephesians*, pp. 395, 397)

Today's Reading

After Christ established this mold, He passed through death
and resurrection, and in resurrection He became the life-giving
Spirit. As such a Spirit, He comes into us to be our life. When we
believed in Him and were baptized, God put us into Him as the
mold, just as dough is placed into a mold. By being put into the mold
we learned the mold;...by being put into Christ, we learn Christ.
On the one hand, God put us into Christ; on the other hand,
Christ has come into us to be our life. Now we may live by Him
according to the mold in which we have been placed by
God....Therefore, with Paul we can say, "To me, to live is Christ"
(Phil. 1:21). We live Christ in the form of His own life, in the form

recorded in the Gospels. (*Life-study of Ephesians,* pp. 397-398)

The reality of the processed Triune God is His consummated Spirit of reality (John 14:17; 15:26; 16:13; 1 John 5:6). The reality of all that the Triune God is, has, and can do is simply this Spirit of reality. The reality of the death and resurrection which the Triune God passed through is also this Spirit of reality.

This Spirit of reality makes everything of the processed Triune God a reality in the Body of Christ (John 16:13-15). It is this same Spirit of reality who makes all the riches of the Triune God, which are just His reality, possible and real in the Body of Christ. All that the processed Triune God is, including righteousness, holiness, life, light, power, grace, and all the divine attributes, are realized by this Spirit of reality to be the real attributes of the Body of Christ (Rom. 15:16b; 14:17; Eph. 3:16).

Furthermore, all that the Triune God experienced, including incarnation, crucifixion, and resurrection, are likewise realized by this Spirit of reality to be the real experiences of the Body of Christ....Because of this we can live a normal human life on the earth today. We can deal with the negative matters which befall us by the capacity of the death of Christ. We do not lose our temper, nor do we blame or rebuke others, because the death of Christ is realized in us through the Spirit of reality. Moreover, the Spirit with the resurrection of Christ works in us to enable us to love and forgive others....This is the Spirit of the reality of the Triune God becoming the reality of the Body of Christ.

This Spirit now dwells in our regenerated Spirit and is joined to our spirit as one spirit (Rom. 8:9-11a; 1 Cor. 6:17)....When we live in this joined spirit, we will be able to live out the Body of Christ and become His corporate expression (Eph. 1:23). (*A Thorough View of the Body of Christ,* pp. 31-33)

Further Reading: Life-study of Ephesians, msg. 46; *The High Peak of the Vision and Reality of the Body of Christ,* chs. 3-4; *A Thorough View of the Body of Christ,* chs. 2-3; *The Practical Points concerning Blending,* ch. 4; *One Body, One Spirit, and One New Man,* ch. 3

Enlightenment and inspiration: _____

_____

_____

_____

Morning Nourishment

Eph. That the God of our Lord Jesus Christ, the Father
1:17 of glory, may give to you a spirit of wisdom and
revelation in the full knowledge of Him.

3:3-4 That by revelation the mystery was made known
to me, as I have written previously in brief, by
which, in reading *it*, you can perceive my understanding in the mystery of Christ.

In Ephesians 1:17 the apostle Paul prayed that the Father
would give us such a mingled spirit of wisdom to understand
and of revelation to see. We need the revelation and the
enlightenment to see the mystery of God's economy. We also
need to understand, to apprehend, what we see by the divine
wisdom. The economy of God is a real mystery, yet it has been
revealed to us. We can see His economy, and it is made known
to us so that we can receive it, understand it, apprehend it,
and participate in it. (*The Issue of the Dispensing of the
Processed Trinity and the Transmitting of the Transcending
Christ,* p. 81)

Today's Reading

The Body of Christ is the continuation of Christ's life on
earth. When He came to the earth and lived on earth, He
expressed Himself through a body. Today He still requires a
body to express Himself. Just as a man needs a body to
express all that he is, Christ needs a body to express Himself.
The function of the Body is to be the full expression of Christ.
We cannot manifest our personality through any one member
of our body—the ears, mouth, eyes, hands, or feet—alone.
Similarly, Christ cannot manifest His personality through
any one member of His Body. It takes His whole Body to manifest Him. We must see that everything of Christ is expressed
through His Body. This is not all. The Body of Christ is the
extension and continuation of Christ on earth. He spent more
than thirty years on earth to reveal Himself. He did this as the

individual Christ. Today He is revealing Himself through the church. This is the corporate Christ. Formerly, Christ was expressed individually; now He is expressed corporately.

The New Testament shows us that there is a difference between being a member and being a Christian. Being a Christian is something individualistic, whereas being a member is something corporate. Being a Christian is something one does for himself, whereas being a member is something for the Body. In the Bible there are many terms with opposite meanings, such as purity and uncleanness, holiness and commonness, victory and defeat, the Spirit and the flesh, Christ and Satan, the kingdom and the world, and glory and shame. All these are opposites. In the same way, the Body is in opposition to the individual. Just as the Father is versus the world, the Spirit is versus the flesh, and the Lord is versus the devil, so also is the Body versus the individual. Once a man sees the Body of Christ, he is free from individualism. He will no longer live for himself but for the Body. Once I am delivered from individualism, I am spontaneously in the Body.

The Body of Christ is not a doctrine; it is a realm. It is not a teaching, but a life. Many Christians seek to teach the truth of the Body, but few know the life of the Body. The Body of Christ is an experience in a totally different realm. A man can know the book of Romans without being justified. Similarly, a man can know the book of Ephesians without seeing the Body of Christ. We do not need knowledge; rather, we need revelation to know the reality of the Body of Christ and to enter the realm of the Body. Only a revelation from God will usher us into the realm of the Body, and only then will the Body of Christ become our experience. (Watchman Nee, *The Mystery of Christ,* pp. 15-17)

Further Reading: The Mystery of Christ, ch. 3; *The Issue of the Dispensing of the Processed Trinity and the Transmitting of the Transcending Christ,* ch. 6

Enlightenment and inspiration: _____

_____

_____

_____

Morning Nourishment

Eph.   The eyes of your heart having been enlightened, that
1:18-19 you may know what is the hope of His calling, and
        what are the riches of the glory of His inheritance in
        the saints, and what is the surpassing greatness of
        His power toward us who believe, according to the
        operation of the might of His strength.

1 Pet.   Blessed be the God and Father of our Lord Jesus
   1:3   Christ, who according to His great mercy has regen-
         erated us unto a living hope through the resurrec-
         tion of Jesus Christ from the dead.

Paul prayed that the eyes of our heart would be enlightened
that we may know three things. The first thing is the hope of God's
calling. The second thing is the riches of the glory of God's inheritance in the saints. That means God in His economy through His
dispensing will get an inheritance, a heritage of worth, and this
heritage will be full of glory. The riches of this glory are unsearch-
able. Paul also prayed that we would know the great surpassing
power that operated in Christ, which is toward us. This is the
power that raised up Christ from the dead, from Hades, that seated
Christ above all things in the heavens, that subjected all things under His feet, and that gave Him to be Head over all things to the
church. This is not common teaching. This is why I have the burden
to stress that we all need to have this prayer. We should pray, "Lord, in
these days in which You are moving in Your recovery on this earth, I
need a spirit of wisdom and of revelation. Lord, give me such a
spirit as a great gift." (*The Issue of the Dispensing of the Processed
Trinity and the Transmitting of the Transcending Christ,* p. 69)

Today's Reading

The hope of God's calling is "Christ in you, the hope of glory"
(Col. 1:27). Christ realized by us, experienced by us, and gained by
us to the fullest extent is the hope of our calling. God called us, justi-
fied us, and He will glorify us, conforming us to the image of His
Son (Rom. 8:29-30). One day we will all be absolutely the same as
Christ (1 John 3:2). Our hope is not just Christ as our Redeemer or

as our life, but Christ as our ultimate manifestation and consummation, as our glory. We are waiting to be fully conformed to the very image of Christ. This is the ultimate consummation of the enjoyment of Christ, and this is the hope of God's calling. (*The Two Greatest Prayers of the Apostle Paul,* p. 12)

[The hope in 1 Peter 1:3 is] a hope for the future in our sojourning today—not a hope of objective things but a hope of life, even eternal life, with all the endless divine blessings. Such a hope should cause us to set our hope perfectly on the coming grace (v. 13).

The living hope, the hope of life, brought to the regenerated believers through regeneration, can be likened to the various expectations for the future brought to parents through the birth of a newborn babe; all such expectations hinge on the life of the newborn child. Likewise, the life that we, the believers, have received through regeneration enables us to have a hope, with numerous aspects, for this age, for the coming age, and for eternity. In this age we have the hope of growing in life, of maturing, of manifesting our gifts, of exercising our functions, of being transformed, of overcoming, of being redeemed in our body, and of entering into glory. In the coming age we have the hope of entering into the kingdom, of reigning with the Lord, and of enjoying the blessings of the eternal life in the manifestation of the kingdom of the heavens. In eternity we have the hope of being in the New Jerusalem, where we will participate fully in the consummated blessings of the eternal life in its ultimate manifestation in eternity. This living hope, the hope of life, hinges on the eternal life, which we received through regeneration. Only the divine life can enable us to grow in the divine life until we grow into the reality of the hope that is brought to us by that life. Thus we will obtain the various blessings mentioned above as our inheritance, which is incorruptible, undefiled, and unfading and is kept for eternity (vv. 3-4). (1 Peter 1:3, note 6)

Further Reading: The Issue of the Dispensing of the Processed Trinity and the Transmitting of the Transcending Christ, ch. 5; Life-study of Ephesians, msg. 15

Enlightenment and inspiration: _____

_____

_____

_____

Morning Nourishment

Eph. ...You may know...what are the riches of the glory
1:18 of His inheritance in the saints.
2 Cor. Since you are being manifested that you are a
3:3 letter of Christ ministered by us, inscribed not
with ink but with the Spirit of the living God; not
in tablets of stone but in tablets of hearts of flesh.

The second matter Paul prays for us to see is the glory of
God's inheritance in the saints (Eph. 1:18). We are always concerned about our own inheritance, but God wants us to care for
His inheritance. God's inheritance in the saints is Christ. The
Christ that has been wrought into each one of us is God's inheritance. Christ is everything. To us, Christ is our hope, and to God,
Christ is His inheritance. There is nothing within us that is
worth being God's inheritance. Only the very Christ who has
been wrought into us can be God's inheritance. We need to ask
how much of Christ has been wrought into us. There may not be
much in us that is good for God to inherit because very little of
Christ has been wrought into us. This is why we need to be
transformed, to have a metabolic change (Rom. 12:2; 2 Cor. 3:18),
and to be conformed to the image of Christ. We all need more of
Christ wrought into our being. The glory of God's inheritance in
the saints is the Christ of glory within us. When we are all transformed and transfigured, conformed to Christ to the uttermost,
God will be happy. All the dear saints will be His inheritance,
and this inheritance will be Christ Himself wrought into all His
believers in full.

The Christ that has been wrought into us is the church, so
the church is God's inheritance. This matter is very deep and
profound. Do not think that the church is an organization, a
group of religious people, or any kind of social or religious entity.
The church is simply Christ wrought into us in a corporate way.
(*The Two Greatest Prayers of the Apostle Paul*, pp. 12-13, 24)

Today's Reading

In 2 Corinthians 3:3 we see the Spirit of the living God as the inscribing ink....God is inscribing Christ into our being, which is like a piece of parchment. In ancient times they did not have paper so they used parchment. You must realize that you are like a piece of parchment, and God is inscribing Christ into your being. This inscribing, however, needs some element, and this element is the transforming Spirit. The transforming Spirit is the inscribing ink used by God as an element to write Christ into your being. God is writing Christ, yet He needs the transforming Spirit as the writing element. Actually and in reality this inscribing ink is just Christ Himself.

The more I write with a pen, the more ink gets onto the paper. What I have written may be a composition, but the element of this composition is ink. God is also writing Christ into our being. The element of His writing is the Spirit of the living God as the inscribing ink. The transforming Spirit is the element, the reality, of Christ. God is writing Christ into us with the transforming Spirit. The transforming Spirit is the element for God to compose Christ, for God to write Christ. Therefore, the composition of Christ is altogether done with the Spirit, and the Spirit is the element of the composition of Christ.

What is on the paper after the writing? Elementary speaking, it is the ink—the Spirit of the living God. Composition wise, it tells us something—Christ. Therefore, the writing ink is the element of Christ. Second Corinthians 3:17 indicates that Christ is the Spirit. Every day the transforming Spirit is being written upon our being as the element, and it manifests Christ. The ink is Christ, and the ink is also the element of Christ. Therefore, the inscribing Spirit, who is the transforming Spirit, is the very element of Christ, even Christ Himself. This is all for transformation. While God is writing with the inscribing Spirit, we are being transformed. (*God's New Testament Economy*, pp. 148-149)

Further Reading: God's New Testament Economy, ch. 13; The Two Greatest Prayers of the Apostle Paul, ch. 1

Enlightenment and inspiration: _____

_____

_____

_____

Morning Nourishment

Eph. In whom you also, having heard the word of the
1:13-14 truth, the gospel of your salvation, in Him also
believing, you were sealed with the Holy Spirit of
the promise, who is the pledge of our inheritance
unto the redemption of the acquired possession, to
the praise of His glory.

4:30 And do not grieve the Holy Spirit of God, in whom
you were sealed unto the day of redemption.

The Spirit is the consummation of the Triune God or the
Triune God consummated....The Triune God has passed
through all the processes, consummating in the Spirit.

In Ephesians the main topic is the Body of Christ, the
church, so in this book the aggregate Spirit, the compound
Spirit, is the Spirit for the Body and the Spirit of the Body. If
there is no Spirit, there is no Body, no church. When people talk
about the Body of Christ, the church, they mostly neglect the
Spirit. Actually, the Spirit is the intrinsic reality of the Body of
Christ. The reality of the church is this compound, aggregate
Spirit. (*God's New Testament Economy*, p. 163)

Today's Reading

Ephesians 1:13 tells us that we believers, who are the com-
ponents, the members of the Body, have all been sealed with
the Holy Spirit. A good example of a seal is a rubber stamp.
When a piece of paper is stamped or sealed, it receives some
element of ink. Now it is no longer purely a piece of paper but a
piece of paper with the element of ink. This shows us that,
firstly, to be sealed is to be impressed with some element. Ephesians 1:13-14 tells us that when we heard the Word and
believed in the Lord Jesus, we were sealed with this compound
Spirit. This sealing put the divine element into our being. This
is just like the stamping of the ink on a piece of paper. It is very
easy to erase something written with pencil. However, when
the best ink is used, it is very hard to erase. Sometimes it
cannot be erased unless you rub through the paper. This means

that the ink element has become one with the paper and that the two elements are mingled as one. In like manner, the divine element has become one with us. The divine Spirit dwells in our human spirit, and these two are mingled together as one spirit (2 Tim. 4:22; Romans 8:16; 1 Cor. 6:17).

In addition, sealing something gives it a mark. To be sealed with the Holy Spirit means to be marked with the Holy Spirit as a living seal. If we had a seal with someone's name on it, the stamping of this seal on a piece of paper would leave the mark of this person's name on the paper. The mark looks exactly the same as the stamp. After we believed in the Lord Jesus, the Holy Spirit sealed us. It not only brought the divine element into our being, but it also put a mark upon us, causing us to bear God's image signified by the seal, thus making us like God.

Sealing also denotes ownership. When a person buys a new book and stamps or seals it with his name, this seal denotes that the book belongs to him. The Holy Spirit put the divine element into our being as a seal to mark us out, indicating that we belong to God. The divine element added into our being, the mark made in us, and the indication of the divine ownership, when added together, become a pledge. A pledge is a guarantee that something is yours. The Holy Spirit sealed upon our being is the pledge that God is ours. It guarantees that God is our inheritance. The members of the church are the sealed ones. All the members have received the Holy Spirit as the divine element, as the divine mark, as the divine ownership, and eventually as a pledge that God is their inheritance. From the day of our salvation we may enjoy God every day as our portion. (*God's New Testament Economy,* pp. 163-165)

Further Reading: God's New Testament Economy, ch. 15; *The Issue of the Dispensing of the Processed Trinity and the Transmitting of the Transcending Christ,* ch. 3; *Life-study of Ephesians,* msgs. 12-13

Enlightenment and inspiration: _____

_____

_____

_____

Morning Nourishment

Eph. And what is the surpassing greatness of His power
1:19-23 toward us who believe, according to the operation of
the might of His strength, which He caused to operate in Christ in raising Him from the dead and seating Him at His right hand in the heavenlies, far
above all rule and authority and power and lordship
and every name that is named not only in this age
but also in that which is to come; and He subjected
all things under His feet and gave Him *to be* Head
over all things to the church, which is His Body, the
fullness of the One who fills all in all.

The third item that Paul prayed for us to see is "the surpassing
greatness of His power" (Eph. 1:19). This is the power which God
has wrought into Christ to do four things: 1) to raise Him from
among the dead (v. 20); 2) to seat Him at the right hand of God
(v. 20); 3) to subject all things under His feet (v. 22); and 4) to
make this Christ the Head over all things to the church (v. 22).
We all have to see the surpassing greatness of this power which
God wrought into Christ. This is the power that overcame death,
the grave, and Hades in raising Jesus from among the dead, that
seated Christ at God's right hand in the heavenlies far above all,
that subjected all things under His feet, and that gave Him to be
Head over all things to the church. This great power is toward us
who believe. We need to know this power because the result, the
issue, the coming forth, of this power is the church. (*The Two
Greatest Prayers of the Apostle Paul,* p. 13)

Today's Reading

The normal, genuine, proper, and real church comes out of this
great power. If you have the power that raised Christ, that seated
Him at God's right hand, far above all, that subjected all things
under His feet, and that gave Him the universal headship, you
have the church. This church is the Body of Christ, "the fullness of
the One who fills all in all" (Eph. 1:23). Christ, who is the infinite,
unlimited God, is so great that He fills all things in all things.

Such a great Christ needs the church to be His fullness for His complete expression. This church comes into being, not from teaching, not from gifts, not from forms, not from rituals, and not from organization, but from the power of the resurrected, ascended, and enthroned Christ, who is now the Head over all things to the church. Ephesians 1:22 does not say that Christ has been made Head over all things *for* the church but *to* the church....."To the church" implies a kind of transmission. Whatever Christ, the Head, attained and obtained is transmitted to the church, His Body. In this transmission the church shares with Christ all His attainments: the resurrection from among the dead, being seated in His transcendency, the subjection of all things under His feet, and the headship over all things. Such a church is Christ's Body, His fullness.

Nothing of our natural life, nature, or makeup, nothing of our natural being, is a part of the church. Only the very portion of Christ that has been wrought into us is a part of the church. Today Christ is in the heavens, yet He is also here on earth. He is like electricity....He is in the heavens, yet He is also within us as the source for us to have the church life. As the heavenly electricity, Christ is being transmitted to the church....God's intention is to work the resurrected, ascended, and enthroned Christ, who is the Head over all things, into us to make us a part of the church. We all need to see the church in this way.

We all need a spirit of wisdom and revelation that we may see these three matters: 1) the hope of God's calling, which is Christ; 2) the glory of God's inheritance in the saints, which is also Christ; and 3) the surpassing greatness of the power that produces the church, the power that raised up Christ, that seated Him in the heavenlies, that put all things under His feet, and that gave Him to be Head over all things to the church. (*The Two Greatest Prayers of the Apostle Paul*, pp. 13-15)

Further Reading: The Two Greatest Prayers of the Apostle Paul,
  ch. 2; *Life-study of Ephesians,* msg. 16

Enlightenment and inspiration: _____

_____

_____

_____

Hymns, #493

1   O Lord, Thou art the Spirit now
That gives us life and quickens us,
With all Thy riches strengthening,
O how divine and glorious!

2   O Lord, Thou art the Spirit now
That with Thy power liberates;
And by Thy liberation true
The law of life now regulates.

3   O Lord, Thou art the Spirit now
That transforms us and saturates,
And to Thine image true conforms
And with Thy light illuminates.

4   O Lord, Thou art the Spirit now
Who in my spirit makes His home;
He mingles with my spirit too,
And both one spirit thus become.

5   Lord, teach me how to exercise
My spirit now to contact Thee,
That in Thy Spirit I may walk
And live by Thy reality.

Composition for prophecy with main point and sub-points: _____

_____

_____

_____

_____

_____

_____

_____

_____

_____

_____

_____

_____

_____

_____

_____

_____

_____

_____

_____

_____

_____

_____

_____

_____

_____

_____

_____

_____

_____

_____

_____

_____

Living in the Mingled Spirit
for the Reality of the Body of Christ
as Revealed in Ephesians
(2)

Scripture Reading: Eph. 2:22; 3:16-21

Day 1 **III. Our spirit is the dwelling place of God; we are "being built together into a dwelling place of God in spirit" (Eph. 2:22):**

A. We should look to the Lord to have mercy on us and to open our eyes to see that the processed and consummated Triune God as the all-inclusive Spirit dwells in our spirit and is mingled with our spirit as one spirit (1 Cor. 15:45b; 2 Cor. 3:17; Rom. 8:16; 1 Cor. 6:17; cf. Rev. 3:18).

B. The most pleasant thing in the eyes of God is that we remain in our spirit, the dwelling place of God; all day long, "in spirit" should govern us and direct all our activities; our highest enjoyment and experience is that the Lord as the Spirit is with our spirit, and we can enjoy Him in our spirit as the presence of grace (Rom. 1:9; 8:16; John 4:24; 2 Cor. 2:13; 2 Tim. 4:22; Gal. 6:18).

Day 2 C. Our regenerated spirit as God's dwelling place, the house of God, is the base on earth where Christ as the heavenly ladder has been set up; hence, whenever we turn to our spirit, we experience Christ as the ladder bringing God into us and us into God for the mingling of God and man (Gen. 28:12-17; John 1:51).

D. Our spirit is the Holy of Holies, the dwelling place of the pneumatic Christ as the embodiment of the Triune God who is typified by the Ark, within which were the hidden manna (signifying God the Father as the divine source of all supply), the budding rod (signifying Christ the Son as the resurrection), and the tablets of the law (signifying the Spirit of life as the inner law of life) (Exo. 25:22; 26:33-34; Heb. 9:3-4; 10:19-22; John 11:25; Rom. 8:2, 16):

Day 3

1. Through our prayer at the incense altar, typifying the resurrected Christ in ascension, we enter into the Holy of Holies— our spirit—where we experience Christ as the Ark of the Testimony with its contents.

2. Through such an experience of Christ in our spirit, we are incorporated into Him to become a part of the corporate Christ as God's testimony for His manifestation (Exo. 38:21; 1 Cor. 12:12).

E. The reality of the church as the Body of Christ is a living in the mingled spirit:

1. Our spirit is where the building up of the church, the dwelling place of God, takes place; the reality of all spiritual things is in the spirit; the church itself is in the spirit, the building of the church is in the spirit, and the eternal testimony of the church is in the spirit (Eph. 2:22).

2. Living in the spirit is the secret and the key to our Christian life and church life; to live in the spirit is to let Christ fill and saturate us until He permeates our whole being and is thereby expressed through us.

Day 4

IV. **Our spirit is our inner man, our new person, our new spirit, our new man; we need to pray to be strengthened with power into the inner man for the reality of the Body life, which is the inner experience of the indwelling Christ as life for God's glory in the church (3:16-21):**

A. In Ephesians 1 our spirit is revealed as an organ for us to receive a revelation concerning the church; in Ephesians 3 our spirit is a person, the inner man, for us to experience Christ for the church; our regenerated spirit, indwelt

by and mingled with the Lord as the Spirit, is
the inner man:

1. Before we were regenerated, our person
   was our soul, our old man; after our regeneration, our new spirit, our new person, our
   new man, is our inner man (Rom. 6:6; Acts
   2:41; Heb. 12:9b; John 3:6; 2 Cor. 4:16; Ezek.
   36:26).

2. The reality of the Body of Christ is the sum
   total of all the new persons within all of us,
   the totality of all our spirits, issuing in one
   great corporate person, one great God-
   man, the Body of Christ as the one new
   man, consummating in the New Jerusalem
   as the new invention and new creation of
   the Triune God (Heb. 12:9b; 2 Cor. 4:16;
   Eph. 2:10, 15; Col. 3:10-11; 2 Cor. 5:17; Gal.
   6:15; Rev. 21:2).

Day 5

B. When we are strengthened into our inner man,
   Christ as the indwelling Spirit in our spirit sup-
   plies, saturates, possesses, and controls every
   part of our heart to become the new person in
   our heart (Eph. 3:16-17).

C. Ephesians 3:17 reveals that the Triune God has
   come into us to do a building work with Himself
   as the element and also with something from us
   as the material; this is illustrated by the parable
   of the sower in Matthew 13:

1. The Lord sows Himself as the seed of life
   into men's hearts, the soil, that He might
   grow and live in them and be expressed
   from within them; the seed is sown into the
   soil to grow with the nutrients of the soil,
   producing a composition of elements from
   both the seed and the soil (vv. 3, 23).

2. We have within us certain nutrients created by God as a preparation for His coming
   into us to grow in us; God has created the
   human spirit with the human nutrients

along with the human heart as the soil for the divine seed (cf. 1 Pet. 3:4).

3. The rate at which we grow in life depends not on the divine seed but on how many nutrients we afford this seed; the more nutrients we supply, the faster the seed will grow and flourish (Psa. 78:8; Matt. 5:3, 8):

   a. If we remain in our soul, in our natural man, there will not be any nutrients for the growth of the divine seed, but if we are strengthened into our inner man and if we pay attention to our spirit and exercise our spirit, the nutrients will be supplied and Christ will make His home in our hearts (Eph. 3:16-17; Rom. 8:6; 1 Tim. 4:7; cf. Jude 19).

   b. In order for the Lord as the seed of life to grow within us to be our full enjoyment, we have to open to the Lord absolutely and cooperate with Him to deal thoroughly with our heart (Matt. 13:3-9, 19-23).

4. On the one hand, God strengthens us with Himself as the element, and on the other hand, we afford the nutrients; through these two God in Christ carries out His intrinsic building—the building of His home—in our entire being.

D. Christ making His home in our hearts causes us to know the knowledge-surpassing love of Christ that we may be filled unto all the fullness of the Triune God for His corporate expression, His glorification (Eph. 3:19-21; cf. Gen. 24:47, 53, 61-67).

Morning Nourishment

Eph. **In whom you also are being built together into a**
2:22 **dwelling place of God in spirit.**
2 Tim. **The Lord be with your spirit. Grace be with you.**
4:22

Song of Songs is a book of figures....The king's inner chambers signify our regenerated spirit as Christ's inner chambers. God created man that man may become Him by His being received by man so that He can enter into and stay in man. For this reason God created us with a spirit. According to the New Testament teaching, our regenerated spirit is not only for us to have a means to receive Him but also for us to contain Him. Second Timothy 4:22 says, "The Lord be with your spirit." Ephesians 3:16 says that we need to be strengthened into our inner man. The inner man is our regenerated spirit. Ephesians 2:22 shows that our spirit is a habitation, a dwelling place, to God. The real inner chambers to God are our spirit. (*Crystallization-study of Song of Songs,* p. 20)

Today's Reading

We should look to the Lord to have mercy on us and to open our eyes that we may see a heavenly vision. We need to see that the great God—Jehovah, the One who is the Father, the Son, and the Spirit, and who is also the Lord Jesus, the Redeemer, the Creator, and the Holy Spirit—is the all-inclusive Spirit who dwells in our spirit and is being mingled with our spirit as one spirit. This is where we should live and walk today. This should not be our performance but our daily living. We should live our daily life in the spirit. We should not be concerned with knowing what humility is or what love is....We should not be concerned with anything other than living in the spirit. We should walk in the spirit day by day, simply being in harmony with our Lord and one with Him in the spirit. We should have our life, nature, living, and walk with our Lord....We do not need to know what it means to love our wife or to submit to our husband. Neither do we need to know what it means to be humble or patient. All these words and phrases are expressions used by moralists....The God and Savior whom we love is the all-inclusive, life-giving Spirit who is dwelling in our spirit and has become one spirit with our spirit. We are joined to Him, and He is our life, our living, and our walk. He and we are one. (*Living in the Spirit,* pp. 28-29)

It is not possible to overstress this matter of the spirit. If we take away from the New Testament these two spirits, the divine and the human, the New Testament becomes empty. Yet Christians pay inaccurate attention to the Holy Spirit and nearly neglect the human spirit. Now is the time when the Lord will recover not only the proper realization of the Holy Spirit, but also the full use of our human spirit.

The most pleasant thing in the eyes of God today is that we remain in our spirit. May we not want to say anything apart from our spirit. May we not want to go anywhere or do anything without being in our spirit. All day long "in spirit" should govern us and direct all our activities. If we speak, think, move, and act in spirit, we are victorious, holy, and spiritual. We shall be pleasant, not only to ourselves, but to God and others as well. Such a daily life is a good pleasure to God. A Christian life and a church life that are in spirit are what pleases Him. (*Life Messages,* pp. 339-340)

[At the end of 2 Timothy], Paul said, "The Lord be with your spirit. Grace be with you" (4:22). If we do not experience the Lord's being with our spirit and therefore lose the presence of grace, that is the degradation of the church. We need to be careful about this. Our highest enjoyment and experience is that our Lord is with our spirit. The Lord, who is the Creator of heaven and earth, the sovereign Lord of all, is with our spirit. This is a tremendous thing. The Lord's being with us is not in our mind or our thoughts; He as the Spirit is with our spirit....Thank the Lord, today the Lord is the Spirit, and we can enjoy Him in the spirit. This is an exceedingly great blessing. To enjoy the Lord's Spirit being in our spirit is to have grace with us. When this is lost, the degradation of the church is present. (*How to Be a Co-worker and an Elder and How to Fulfill Their Obligations,* p. 45)

Further Reading: Living in the Spirit, ch. 2; *Life Messages,* ch. 38

Enlightenment and inspiration: _____

_____

_____

_____

Morning Nourishment

Gen.   And he dreamed that there was a ladder set up on the
28:12 earth, and its top reached to heaven; and there the
       angels of God were ascending and descending on it.
   18 And Jacob rose up early in the morning and took the
       stone that he had put under his head, and he set it up
       as a pillar and poured oil on top of it.
Heb.   Let us therefore come forward with boldness to the
4:16   throne of grace that we may receive mercy and find
       grace for timely help.

Eventually, [in Genesis 28] Jacob poured oil, a symbol of the
Spirit as the consummation of the Triune God reaching man (Exo.
30:23-30; Luke 4:18), on the pillar, symbolizing that the transformed man is one with the Triune God and expresses Him. That
stone became Bethel, the house of God (Gen. 28:19, 22). God's
house is the mutual dwelling place of God and His redeemed (John
14:2, 23)—man as God's dwelling place (Isa. 66:1-2; 1 Cor. 3:16;
Eph. 2:22; Heb. 3:6; Rev. 21:3) and God as man's dwelling place
(Psa. 90:1; John 15:5; Rev. 21:22). Hence, the house of God is constituted of God and man mingled together as one. In God's house God
expresses Himself in humanity, and both God and man find
mutual and eternal satisfaction and rest. (Gen. 28:12, note 1)

Today's Reading

[The ladder in Genesis 28:12] is the center, the focus, of Jacob's
dream. This dream is a revelation of Christ, for Christ is the reality of the ladder that Jacob saw (John 1:51 and notes). Christ as
the Son of Man, in His humanity, is the ladder that brings heaven
(God) to earth (man) and joins earth and heaven as one (cf. John
14:6). Our regenerated spirit, which is God's dwelling place today
(Eph. 2:22), is the base on earth where Christ as the heavenly ladder has been set up (2 Tim. 4:22). Hence, whenever we turn to our
spirit, we experience Christ as the ladder bringing God to us and
us to God (see note 1 on Heb. 10:19). Where this ladder is, there
are an open heaven, the transformed man, the anointing upon
this man, and the building up of the house of God with this man.

The issue of Christ as the heavenly ladder is Bethel, the church, the Body of Christ, and the consummation of this ladder is the New Jerusalem. (Gen. 28:12, note 2)

We preach the pneumatic Christ, the Christ who is the Spirit (2 Cor. 3:17). This One is private and spiritual. We have seen that the king's chambers signify our spirit. He visits us in our spirit privately, and He comes to us in a spiritual way, not a physical way. He visits us privately as the all-inclusive, consummated Spirit.

Christ the King brings His seekers into His chambers, that is into their regenerated spirit, His dwelling place. Let us consider the application of this. When I was young, I was taught to pray to God as the heavenly Father. I was also told not to pray to the Spirit, because in the entire New Testament you cannot find a verse concerning praying to the Spirit. But the more we pray, the more we have the feeling that the Father, the Son, and the Spirit are all in us (Eph. 4:6; 2 Cor. 13:5; Rom. 8:9). According to our experience, our spirit is the Holy of Holies—the dwelling place, the inner chambers, of the Triune God.

The seeker in Song of Songs prayed, "Draw me; we will run after you." Then the king drew her and she followed, but she did not know where to go. The King knows where to go. We must go to our spirit. The inner chambers of Christ are His lovers' regenerated spirits mingled with and indwelt by Him as the life-dispensing Spirit (Rom. 8:16; 2 Tim. 4:22; Rom. 8:11) and are the practical Holy of Holies in Christ's lovers for their participation in and enjoyment of the pneumatic Christ as the consummated Triune God (Heb. 4:16).

After we were saved we began to pray,...[and] gradually we found out that the Triune God dwells in our regenerated spirit. The seeker followed the Lord, and He immediately brought her to her regenerated spirit to have fellowship with Him. (*Crystallization-study of Song of Songs*, p. 21)

Further Reading: Life-study of John, msgs. 4-5; *Crystallization-study of Song of Songs,* msg. 2

Enlightenment and inspiration: _____

_____

_____

_____

Morning Nourishment

Heb. **And after the second veil, a tabernacle, which is**
9:3-4 **called the Holy of Holies, having a golden altar and**
the Ark of the Covenant covered about every-
where with gold, in which were the golden pot that
had the manna and Aaron's rod that budded and
the tablets of the covenant.
10:22 **Let us come forward to *the Holy of Holies*...**

The Holy of Holies today is in heaven, where the Lord Jesus is (Heb. 9:12, 24). Then, how can we enter it while we are still on earth? The secret is our spirit, referred to in 4:12. The very Christ who is in heaven is also now in our spirit (2 Tim. 4:22). He, as the heavenly ladder (Gen. 28:12; John 1:51), joins our spirit to heaven and brings heaven into our spirit. Whenever we turn to our spirit, we enter into the Holy of Holies. Here we meet with God who is on the throne of grace. (*Life-study of Hebrews*, p. 490)

Today's Reading

The veil is the separation in God's dwelling place, His sanctuary. God's sanctuary is one, but it is separated by a veil. At one end is the Holy Place, and at the other end is the Holy of Holies where God Himself dwells in His Divine Trinity.

Within the Ark in the Holy of Holies there were three items: the hidden manna, the budding rod, and the tablets of the law (Heb. 9:4). The hidden manna in the golden pot refers to God the Father as the divine source of all supply, and the budding rod signifies Christ as the resurrection. Among the three of the Divine Trinity, the second is the resurrection. Jesus told us that He is the resurrection (John 11:25), the reality of the budding rod of Aaron. The tablets of the law refer to the Spirit of life as the inner law (Rom. 8:2). Thus, the Father, the Son, and the Spirit are dwelling in the Holy of Holies. When we enter into the Holy of Holies, we enter into God and meet the Father as the source of supply, the Son as the resurrection, and the Spirit as the law of life. (*Crystallization-study of Song of Songs*, p. 109)

[The two altars mentioned in Psalm 84:3 are] the bronze altar for the sacrifices and the golden altar of incense. The two altars signify the leading consummations of the work of the incarnated Triune God, who is Christ as the embodiment of God for His increase. The mentioning of these two altars together in Exo. 40:5-6 indicates that they are closely related in our spiritual experience. At the bronze altar, a type of the cross of Christ, our problems before God are solved through the crucified Christ as the sacrifices. This qualifies us to enter into the tabernacle, a type of Christ as the incarnated and enterable Triune God, and to contact God at the incense altar. At the golden altar of incense in front of the Holy of Holies (see note 1 on Heb. 9:4), the resurrected Christ in His ascension is the incense for us to be accepted by God in peace. Through our prayer at the incense altar we enter into the Holy of Holies—our spirit (Heb. 10:19)—where we experience Christ as the Ark of the Testimony with its contents. Through such an experience of Christ we are incorporated into the tabernacle, the incarnated Triune God, to become a part of the corporate Christ (1 Cor. 12:12) as God's testimony for His manifestation. (Psa. 84:3, note 1)

If the Lord is merciful to open your eyes and show you this matter, your entire Christian life will have a great turn....Ultimately, the entire Bible requires only one thing of us—to walk according to the mingled spirit, which is the all-inclusive Spirit mingled with our regenerated spirit...."He who is joined to the Lord is one spirit." If our disposition is manifested, this proves that we are not in spirit. If we criticize and judge carelessly, this also proves that we are not in spirit....Then what does it mean to be in spirit? To be in spirit is simply to be in spirit, and to not be in spirit is simply to not be in spirit. We need to see that the reality of all spiritual things is in the spirit. The church itself is in the spirit, the building of the church is in the spirit, and the eternal testimony of the church is in the spirit. This is the hinge, the secret, and the key to our Christian life and our church life. (*Living in the Spirit*, p. 29)

Further Reading: Life-study of Hebrews, msgs. 39-40, 44; Crystallization-study of Song of Songs, msg. 12

Enlightenment and inspiration: _____

_____

_____

_____

Morning Nourishment

Eph. That the God of our Lord Jesus Christ, the Father
1:17 of glory, may give to you a spirit of wisdom and
revelation in the full knowledge of Him.
3:16 That He would grant you, according to the riches of
His glory, to be strengthened with power through
His Spirit into the inner man.
Heb. ...Shall we not much more be in subjection to the
12:9 Father of spirits and live?

In Paul's first prayer [in Ephesians], the key is our spirit. Now
in the second prayer, the key is the inner man. The spirit is for our
seeing, for the revelation, and the inner man is for the experience.
Our spirit is for us to use as an organ to see the things of the church,
but the inner man is not just an organ. The inner man is a person.
By this person, we can experience Christ that the church may come
into being. Actually, the inner man is simply our spirit with something added. When Christ as life comes into our spirit, it becomes a
person. The inner man is our regenerated person with God's life as
its life. (*The Two Greatest Prayers of the Apostle Paul*, p. 29)

Today's Reading

We all have to see the difference between the spirit as an organ
and the inner man. According to 1 Thessalonians 5:23, man is of
three parts: spirit, soul, and body. Our soul is our human life. This
is why in the New Testament, the same Greek word *psuche* is
translated "soul" in some cases (Luke 12:20; Acts 2:43) and "life"
in others (Luke 12:22-23; John 12:25). Because our human life is
in our soul, our soul is our person, our being, and our self....A soul
is a person because a human being's life is in the soul, but the
spirit by itself is merely an organ. Just as our body is an outward
organ to contact the outward, physical world, our spirit is an
inward organ to contact the spiritual world. Before being saved,
each of us was a soul, a being, a person, with two organs: the body
as an outward organ and the spirit as an inward organ. But now
Christ has come into our spirit as life, and this life is not *psuche,*
the soul-life, but the divine life. Whenever the New Testament in

the original Greek speaks of this life, it always uses the word *zoe* (John 1:4; 1 John 1:2; 5:12). *Zoe* is the divine, eternal, uncreated life of God, which is Christ Himself. Christ is our life in our spirit (Col. 3:4; Rom. 8:10). Without this life, our spirit would only be an organ, not a person. As saved ones with Christ as life in our spirit, our spirit has become a man, a person, a being. It is not merely an inward organ, but it is now an inner man. This is the inner man referred to by Paul in Ephesians 3:16.

Before we were saved, we had only one life, the soul-life, but now we have another life, the divine life in our spirit. Because we now have two lives, we have a problem. By which of these lives will we live? If we live by the soul-life, *psuche,* we will be soulish, but if we live by the divine life, *zoe,* we will be spiritual. We should all desire to live by the life in our spirit, by the new divine life, *zoe,* and not by the old human life, *psuche.*

In Ephesians 1 our spirit is revealed as an organ for us to receive revelation concerning the church. In Ephesians 3 our spirit is a person, the inner man, for us to experience Christ for the church. Because chapter one refers to our need to see the spiritual revelation, it reveals the spirit as an organ. Chapter three shows us that we have to live according to what we have seen. For this we need the inner man, a person. As a person, our spirit is for us to live by and for us to experience what we have seen.

May the Lord open our eyes to see that the church life is in this new person and nothing else. Regardless of how good, patient, humble, kind, and mild you are, as long as you are in the old person, you cannot experience the church life....The church life is absolutely something in the new person. There is a new person within each of us. All of these new persons added together equals the church. What is the church? The church is the summation, the sum total, of all the new persons within us. The church life is in our spirit. (*The Two Greatest Prayers of the Apostle Paul,* pp. 29-30, 43)

Further Reading: The Two Greatest Prayers of the Apostle Paul, chs. 3-4

Enlightenment and inspiration: _____

_____

_____

_____

Morning Nourishment

Eph. 3:17 That Christ may make His home in your hearts through faith...

John 14:23 Jesus...said to him, If anyone loves Me, he will keep My word, and My Father will love him, and We will come to him and make an abode with him.

Matt. 13:23 But the one sown on the good earth, this is he who hears the word and understands, who by all means bears fruit and produces, one a hundredfold, and one sixtyfold, and one thirtyfold.

[Paul prays that God would strengthen the believers "with power through His Spirit into the inner man" (Eph. 3:16).] The issue of this strengthening is "that Christ may make His home in your hearts" (v. 17). Not only is Christ in our spirit, but also, as a person, He must inhabit our whole inward being, our heart. The heart is composed of the three parts of the soul—the mind (Matt. 9:4; Heb. 4:12), the emotion (John 16:6, 22), and the will (Acts 11:23; Heb. 4:12)—plus the conscience (Heb. 10:22; 1 John 3:20), a part of the spirit. The heart includes all our inward parts. This means that when we are strengthened into our inner man, Christ will take over our entire inward being. When we are strengthened into our inner man, into our spirit, it will be easy for Christ as the indwelling Spirit to saturate every inward part of our being...[and] take over our mind, our emotion, and our will. Then Christ can settle down in our being, making His home in our hearts. (*The Two Greatest Prayers of the Apostle Paul*, p. 33)

Today's Reading

The Bible tells us that God is working in us and that Christ is living in us. However, the Bible uses a very striking term—*build*—to denote God's work in us. In Ephesians 3:16-17 Paul prayed....The words "that Christ may make His home" are a strong indication that He is doing a work of building in us. Christ is building a home in our inner being.

In order to build a home in us, Christ must have the material. On the one hand, this material is Christ Himself as the element;

on the other hand, this material includes something from us with our humanity....The Triune God has come into us to do a building work with Himself as the element and also with something from us as the material....God's building Himself in Christ into us has very much to do with what we are.

This is illustrated by the parable of the sower in Matthew 13. The seed is sown into the soil to grow with the nutrients in the soil. This seed, therefore, does not grow just with itself; it grows with itself and the nutrients in the soil. As a result, the produce is a composition of elements from both the seed and the soil. Here we see an important spiritual principle. In order to grow, the seed must be sown into good soil. If the seed were sown into sand or among stones, it would not grow, because neither sand nor stone can supply the necessary nutrients.

In Matthew 13 the seed is divinity, and the soil with its nutrients is humanity. We have within us certain nutrients created by God as a preparation for His coming into us to grow in us. God has created the human spirit with the human nutrients. For this reason, human beings can believe in the Lord and receive Him.

The seed that has been sown into us is Christ as the embodiment of the Triune God. The rate at which the seed grows within us depends on the nutrients afforded by us. The more nutrients we supply, the faster the seed will grow and the more it will flourish....[The] building takes place by the growth of the divine seed within us.

The Triune God, the source of life, has sown Himself in Christ as a seed into our being. Once this seed comes into us, it meets something within us—our spiritual nutrients—and it begins to grow. The degree of growth depends not on the divine seed but on how many nutrients we afford this seed. Matthew 13 indicates that only the good soil (vv. 8, 23) affords the adequate nutrients for the growth of the divine seed. (*Life-study of 1 & 2 Samuel,* pp. 196-197)

Further Reading: Life-study of 1 & 2 Samuel, msg. 30; *Life Messages,* ch. 37

Enlightenment and inspiration: _____
_____
_____
_____

Morning Nourishment

Eph. **And to know the knowledge-surpassing love of**
3:19-21 **Christ, that you may be filled unto all the fullness**
of God. But to Him who is able to do superabun-
dantly above all that we ask or think, according to
the power which operates in us, to Him be the
glory in the church and in Christ Jesus unto all the
generations forever and ever. Amen.

Since God's building Himself in Christ into us depends not only
on Himself as the element but also on the nutrients supplied by us,
we need to be strengthened into our inner man. If we remain in our
soul, in our natural man, there will not be any nutrients for the
growth of the divine seed. But if we are strengthened into our inner
man and if we pay attention to our spirit and exercise our spirit, the
nutrients will be supplied. Then Christ will make His home in our
inner being. (*Life-study of 1 & 2 Samuel,* p. 198)

Today's Reading

If Christ's making His home in our hearts did not need something from us, Paul would not have prayed…that the Father
would strengthen us with power through His Spirit into our inner
man. This power, referred to in Ephesians 1:19-22, is the power
that raised Christ from the dead, seated Christ at the right hand
of God in the heavenlies, subjected all things under Christ's feet,
and gave Christ to be Head over all things to the church. Such
power operates in us (3:20), and with it God strengthens us for
His building. The Spirit through whom God strengthens us is the
consummation of the processed Triune God. On the one hand,
God strengthens us with Himself as the element and, on the other
hand, we afford the nutrients. Through these two God in Christ
carries out His intrinsic building—the building of His home—in
our entire being. (*Life-study of 1 & 2 Samuel,* p. 198)

We have seen that the Lord's intention is to sow Himself as the
seed of life into us. We are the living earth, the living soil, the living
ground. The spirit is enclosed by the heart, so if the Lord is going
to come into us, our heart has to be opened. We can open our heart

to the Lord by repenting and confessing....To repent means to turn, ...to open our mind. Following this our conscience will be exercised in a thorough confession of our sins. Then our emotion will follow to love the Lord and our will will follow to choose the Lord. The result will be that our heart will be fully opened to the Lord, and the Lord will have a way to fill us with Himself. This is the way to deal with our heart to make it the good ground for the Lord as the seed of life to grow in. (*The Tree of Life*, pp. 124-125)

We all need to see the vision of how the church is constituted. How we need to be strengthened into our inner man! Every fiber of our being needs to be strengthened into our inner man. Not one part of our inward being should remain in a weak condition. We need to be strengthened so that the indwelling Christ can spread Himself throughout our being and make His home in our inward parts. As Christ spreads within us, He saturates every area of our inner being metabolically with all that He is. Then we are rooted and grounded in love, we lay hold of the dimensions of Christ, and we know His love that surpasses knowledge. Then, ultimately, we are filled unto the fullness of God which is the church. What a high revelation of the church this is!

The Body of Christ is the expression of Christ. It is also the fullness of Christ, which is the fullness of God. This fullness of God comes into existence in a practical way by our being strengthened into the inner man, by Christ making His home in our hearts, by our being rooted and grounded in love, by our grasping the dimensions of the immeasurable Christ, and by our knowing Him as the knowledge-surpassing love. When we have been filled with all the riches of Christ and metabolically saturated with all that Christ is, we become the fullness of God. Surely this is the highest definition of the church....Now that the church has come into existence in a practical way, Christ can be glorified in the church [v. 21]. (*Life-study of Ephesians*, pp. 294-296)

Further Reading: The Tree of Life, ch. 13; The Way to Build Up the Church; Life-study of Ephesians, msg. 34

Enlightenment and inspiration: _____

_____

_____

_____

Hymns, #1134

1   Oh, strengthen my spirit, Lord Jesus,
     Oh, strengthen my spirit, I pray;
     Oh, strengthen my spirit with power
     And spread to my heart today.

       Into my heart, into my heart,
       Spread into my heart, Lord Jesus;
       Make home today and have Your way
       In all of my heart, Lord Jesus.

2   Spread into my heart, O Lord Jesus,
     Spread into my heart, I pray;
     Spread into my heart from my spirit,
     Spread into my heart today.

3   Make home in my heart, O Lord Jesus,
     Make home in my heart, I pray;
     That we may be filled with Your fullness,
     Make home in my heart today.

4   To Him who is able to do it
     Above all we think or say,
     We open our hearts wide and welcome
     Him into our heart today.

Composition for prophecy with main point and sub-points: _____

Living in the Mingled Spirit
for the Reality of the Body of Christ
as Revealed in Ephesians
(3)

Scripture Reading: Eph. 4:3-4, 23-24; 5:18-21; 6:17-18

Day 1 **V. We must allow the renewing Spirit mingled with our regenerated spirit to become the spirit of our mind so that we can be renewed day by day to become as new as the New Jerusalem for the reality of the Body of Christ as the new man (Titus 3:5; Eph. 4:23-24; 2 Cor. 4:16; Col. 3:10-11):**

A. Our mingled spirit needs to spread into our mind in order to subdue, take over, and occupy our mind, thus becoming the spirit of our mind; the more the mingled spirit penetrates, saturates, and possesses our mind, the more we let Christ's mind become our mind (Phil. 2:5; Eph. 4:23; 1 Cor. 2:16).

B. To be renewed in the spirit of our mind is to get rid of all the old concepts concerning the things of the human life and to be made new again by the teaching of the Holy Scriptures and the enlightening of the Holy Spirit; this renewing is carried out by the exercise of our spirit in prayer and in reading the Word day by day (Psa. 119:105, 130; 2 Tim. 3:15-17; Deut. 17:18-20).

Day 2 C. Our being renewed in the spirit of our mind is for our daily transformation into the image of Christ through the consuming of our outer man by the suffering in our environment for the renewing of our inner man by the fresh supply of the pneumatic Christ as the resurrection life (Rom. 12:2; 2 Cor. 3:18; 4:16).

D. We should not live according to the vanity of the mind but according to the spirit of the mind; this is the key to the daily living of the corporate one

new man, the secret to having a church life filled
with the character of God, the aroma of Christ,
and the oneness of the Spirit (Eph. 4:3-4, 17-18,
23-24).

Day 3 VI. **We must be filled with the beautifying,
bride-preparing Spirit mingled with our
spirit so that we can be prepared to be
Christ's glorious church, His beautiful bride
and the house of God's beauty, for God's
expression (5:18, 26-27; Isa. 60:7, 19; 62:3;
Gen. 1:26):**

A. We must be filled in our spirit with Christ as the
beautifying Spirit unto all the fullness of God
(Eph. 5:18; 3:19):

1. To be drunk with wine in the body dissi-
pates us, but to be filled in spirit causes
us to overflow with Christ in speaking,
singing, psalming, giving thanks to God,
and subjecting ourselves to one another
(5:18-21).

2. Out of this inward filling will come submis-
sion, love, obedience, care, and all the other
virtues of a proper Christian life, church
life, family life, and community life for the
expression of Christ in His Body with the
glory of His divinity and the beauty of His
humanity (5:22—6:9; cf. Exo. 28:2).

Day 4 B. We must be beautified by Christ as the life-
giving, speaking Spirit in our spirit; through the
Lord's speaking within us as the life-giving
Spirit, we are becoming His glorious church
(Eph. 5:26-27; Rev. 2:7):

1. The primary work of the Lord in His recovery is for Him to prepare His glorious bride;
the beauty of the bride comes from the very
Christ who is wrought into the church and
expressed through the church (19:7-9;
cf. Isa. 28:5; Psa. 27:4).

2. The church is being beautified through the

process of sanctification by Christ as the life-giving Spirit cleansing us by the washing of the water in His word (Eph. 5:26):

a. This indicates that in the word of Christ is the Spirit as the water of life; the words that He speaks to us are spirit and life (John 6:63).

b. The Greek word rendered "word" in Ephesians 5:26 is not *logos,* the constant word, but *rhema,* which denotes the instant word, the word the Lord presently speaks to us.

c. Christ's speaking is the Spirit; His speaking is the very presence of the life-giving Spirit (John 6:63; Eph. 6:17).

d. The indwelling Christ as the life-giving Spirit is always speaking an instant, present, living word to metabolically cleanse away the old and replace it with the new, causing an inward transformation.

3. Through such a washing process, we are saturated with Christ and beautified by Christ to be His holy, beautiful, God-expressing bride, a bride without blemish or imperfection (Rev. 19:7; cf. S. S. 6:13; 8:13-14).

Day 5 & Day 6 **VII. We must experience the slaying Spirit mingled with our spirit so that everything of God's adversary can be killed within us, enabling us to rule in the divine life of the Spirit over Satan, sin, and death for God's dominion (Eph. 6:17-18; Rom. 5:17; Gen. 1:26):**

A. In Ephesians 5 the word is for nourishment, which leads to the beautifying of the bride, but in Ephesians 6 the word is for killing, which enables the church as the corporate warrior to engage in spiritual warfare (vv. 10-18).

    B. We must receive the word of God by means of
all prayer, "praying at every time in spirit"
(vv. 17-18):

      1. We need to receive the word of God in a
living way, that is, to receive the word as the
Spirit; then the Spirit becomes the killing
sword to kill all the "germs" within us and
the evil spirits in the air so that we can live
a healthy Body life, a healthy church life.

      2. Without the word as the Spirit to be the
killing sword, there would be no way for us
to be kept in the church life over the years.

      3. When we exercise our spirit to pray over
and with God's word, His word slays the
adversary in us, killing the negative elements within us, such as hatred, jealousy,
pride, and doubts; as we pray-read the
word, eventually the self, the worst foe of all
and the enemy of the Body, will be put to
death, and Christ will be victorious in our
entire being.

**VIII. We must live in our mingled spirit for the
reality of the Body of Christ so that the Lord
can recover the "missed" Body of Christ and
the "neglected" oneness of the Body of
Christ; to live in our mingled spirit and in
the unique oneness of the Body, as revealed
in the book of Ephesians, is to be kept in the
Lord's recovery (John 4:24; Eph. 4:3-4, 23).**

Morning Nourishment

Rom. **And do not be fashioned according to this age, but**
12:2 **be transformed by the renewing of the mind that**
you may prove what the will of God is, that which
is good and well pleasing and perfect.
Eph. **...Be renewed in the spirit of your mind.**
4:23

The way to put on the new man is for our spirit (which is mingled with the Spirit), in which are found God, God's dwelling place, and the new man, to become the spirit of our mind. Our mind dominates and directs our whole being. For the spirit to become the spirit of our mind means that the spirit directs, controls, dominates, and possesses our mind....When the spirit directs our mind, it governs our whole being. When this is the case, our being is under the control of our spirit, in which are found God, the dwelling place of God, and the new man. It is in this spirit of our mind that we are renewed. By means of this spirit we put on the new man.

How much we put on the new man depends on how much our spirit directs our being. When our spirit dominates and directs us, there is no ground for opinions or ordinances. There is no room for our way, because our whole being is dominated, controlled, governed, and directed by our spirit. (*Life-study of Ephesians*, pp. 213-214)

Today's Reading

Putting on the new man does not take place once for all. On the contrary, it is a lifelong matter, a gradual process that goes on throughout our Christian life....The new man has been created in Christ and with Christ. [Ephesians 2:15 says that Christ created the new man "in Himself."]...The Greek word rendered "in" has an instrumental significance; it also means "with." Thus, in Himself actually means with Himself. The new man has already been created with Christ as the divine essence. When we were regenerated, this new man was put into our spirit. Now day by day we need to put on this new man by permitting the spirit to control our being and renew our mind. Every time part of our being is renewed, we put on a little more of the new man. Hence, the more we are renewed through the spirit controlling our mind, the more of the new man we put on. Eventually, this process of putting on the new man will be completed. (*Life-study of Ephesians*, pp. 214-215)

The renewing taught by the Scriptures is the renewing of the mind; it is altogether a matter related to the mind. The mind is our mentality, our philosophy, our religious concepts, our views concerning people and things, etc. We need to be renewed mainly in our mind.

[In] Ephesians 4:23...the spirit of our mind is the regenerated spirit mingled with the Spirit of God spreading into our mind to exercise control over it. In this way our mind is renewed. Furthermore, Romans 8:6 says, "...the mind set on the spirit is life and peace." This also shows us the importance of our mind. Our mind can be renewed only by our setting it on the spirit.

Not only so, the New Testament teaches us to have the mind in us which was also in Christ Jesus (Phil. 2:5). This is equivalent to taking the mind of Christ Jesus as our mind. By regeneration we have the life of God, by sanctification we partake of the nature of God, and by renewing we have a change in our mind.

How can our mind be renewed that our whole being may be renewed? The way of renewing lies in prayer and in reading the Scriptures, because for us to be renewed in our mind is for us to get rid of all our old concepts concerning the things of the human life and be made new again by the teaching of the Holy Scriptures and the enlightening of the Holy Spirit. When you read the Bible and become familiar with it, the Holy Spirit will enlighten you and guide you. When the Holy Spirit comes to enlighten you while you thus pray and read the Word day by day, the mind in you is being changed from the old to the new. Your view is different and your being is renewed. (*The Organic Aspect of God's Salvation*, pp. 44-45)

Further Reading: The Organic Aspect of God's Salvation, ch. 3; Life-study of Ephesians, msg. 69; Incarnation, Inclusion, and Intensification, ch. 4

Enlightenment and inspiration: _____
_____
_____
_____

Morning Nourishment

2 Cor. **Therefore we do not lose heart; but though our**
4:16 **outer man is decaying, yet our inner *man* is being**
      renewed day by day.
Eph. **This therefore I say and testify in the Lord, that**
4:17 **you no longer walk as the Gentiles also walk in**
      the vanity of their mind.
   23 **And *that* you be renewed in the spirit of your**
      mind.

Renewing takes place through the consuming by the believers' environmental suffering (2 Cor. 4:16). This suffering kills the believers' outer man and renews their inner man day by day. Human life is more a life of suffering than a life of enjoyment. Much of the believers' environmental suffering is related to their family life, to their daily life with their spouse, children, and relatives. Our environment is according to God's sovereign arrangement, and we cannot escape it. God arranges our environment so that little by little and day by day our outer man will be consumed and our inner man will be renewed. (*The Secret of God's Organic Salvation: "The Spirit Himself with Our Spirit,"* p. 38)

Today's Reading

In the church as the new man, we should live not according to the vanity of the mind, but according to the spirit of the mind (Eph. 4:23). This is the key to the daily living of the corporate one new man. Formerly, our mind was filled with vanity; now it must be permeated with the spirit. We need to walk according to the spirit that is spreading into our mind and filling it. In this way the daily walk of the new man will be in the spirit of the mind. This is the secret of the church life.

As we go on to chapter four, we see that the strengthened spirit must become the renewing spirit in our mind. In 4:23 Paul says, "And that you be renewed in the spirit of your mind." Once again, the spirit here is the regenerated spirit of the believers mingled with the indwelling Spirit of God. Such a mingled spirit spreads into our mind and thereby becomes the spirit of our mind. It is in such a spirit that we are renewed for our transformation (Rom. 12:2; 2 Cor. 3:18).

Our strengthened spirit is the means for our entire being to be renewed. When our spirit has become strong, it will spread into our mind and cause it to be renewed. When our spirit renews our mind, it proceeds to renew our emotion and our will. By such a renewing spirit the church has the proper living as the one new man.

In Ephesians 4:24 Paul says that the new man was created according to God in righteousness and holiness of the truth. Righteousness is a matter of being right with God and man according to God's righteous way; holiness is a matter of being separated unto God from anything common and of being saturated with God's holy nature.

The key to the church life is the spirit of the mind. If we live according to the spirit of the mind, there will be in the church life the expression of the divine character. Then we shall be a corporate people with the flavor of Christ and the expression of God. If we simply give others the impression that we are good, righteous, and kind, our church life is a failure. There must be in our goodness, righteousness, and kindness the expression of the Triune God. The church life must be filled with the aroma and flavor of Christ and with the character of God. Such a living is the living of the Triune God through our humanity. For centuries, God has been longing for such a church life. We pray that before long this kind of church life will be fully practiced among us in the Lord's recovery. May the Lord be satisfied by seeing such an expression of Himself through the corporate new man on earth! (*Life-study of Ephesians,* pp. 783-784, 786, 790, 792-793)

Further Reading: Life-study of Ephesians, msg. 94; *The Secret of God's Organic Salvation:* "*The Spirit Himself with Our Spirit,*" ch. 3

Enlightenment and inspiration: _____

_____

_____

_____

Morning Nourishment

Eph. And do not be drunk with wine, in which is disso-
5:18-21 luteness, but be filled in spirit, speaking to one
another in psalms and hymns and spiritual songs,
singing and psalming with your heart to the Lord,
giving thanks at all times for all things in the name
of our Lord Jesus Christ to *our* God and Father,
being subject to one another in the fear of Christ.

3:19 And to know the knowledge-surpassing love of
Christ, that you may be filled unto all the fullness
of God.

We need to go on from the function in Ephesians 4 to the
beauty in Ephesians 5. In caring for their children, mothers
may value strength in a boy, but they appreciate beauty in a
girl. Likewise, in the church as the one new man there is
strength and ability, but with the church as the bride there is
beauty and glory. We should learn somewhat to depreciate our
ability and strength, for as part of the bride, we shall be not
male, but female. At the time of the wedding, what the church
will need is beauty, not strength. Oh, the church is being beautified by partaking of Christ, by digesting Christ, and by
assimilating Christ! The more we experience the indwelling
Christ in this way, the more He will replace our spots and
wrinkles with His element, and the more His riches with the
divine attributes will become our beauty. Then we shall be
prepared to be presented to Christ as His lovely bride.
(*Life-study of Ephesians,* p. 801)

Today's Reading

In Ephesians 5:18 Paul says, "And do not be drunk with
wine, in which is dissoluteness, but be filled in spirit." To be
drunk with wine is to be filled in the body, whereas to be filled
in our regenerated spirit is to be filled with Christ (1:23) unto
the fullness of God (3:19). To be drunk with wine in the body
causes us to be dissipated, but to be filled with Christ unto the
fullness of God causes us to overflow with Him in speaking,

singing, psalming, giving thanks to God, and subjecting ourselves one to another. Day by day we need to be filled in our
spirit with the riches of Christ.

Verses 19 through 21 are related to "be filled in spirit" in
verse 18. Psalms, hymns, and spiritual songs are not only for
singing and psalming, but also for speaking to one another.
Such speaking, singing, and psalming are not only the outflow
of being filled in spirit, but also the way to be filled in spirit.
Psalms are long poems, hymns are shorter ones, and spiritual
songs are the shortest. All are needed in order for us to be
filled with the Lord and to overflow with Him in our Christian
life.

Being subject to one another [in verse 21] is also the way to
be filled in spirit with the Lord and also the overflow of being
filled. Our subjection should be one to another, not only the
younger ones to the older ones, but also the older ones to the
younger ones (1 Pet. 5:5).

The life of speaking, singing, psalming, and thanking is a
life of subjection. When we speak, sing, psalm, and give
thanks in the name of the Lord Jesus Christ, we are willing to
submit ourselves to one another. We all submit to Christ the
Head and also to the Body. But this submitting comes from
the speaking, the singing, the psalming, and the giving of
thanks, which in turn come from the infilling. When we are
filled in our spirit, we sing, we psalm, we speak, and we thank.
Spontaneously, we also submit. However, if we are not filled,
there will be no speaking, singing, psalming, or thanking God,
and consequently there will be no submitting. The proper
church people are those who are submissive by speaking,
singing, psalming, and giving thanks to God from their inner
being. They live in the way of being filled in spirit with all the
riches of Christ unto the fullness of God. (*Life-study of Ephesians,* pp. 434-436)

Further Reading: Life-study of Ephesians, msg. 51

Enlightenment and inspiration: _____
_____
_____
_____

Morning Nourishment

Eph. Husbands, love your wives even as Christ also
5:25-27 loved the church and gave Himself up for her that
He might sanctify her, cleansing *her* by the washing of the water in the word, that He might present
the church to Himself glorious, not having spot or
wrinkle or any such things, but that she would be
holy and without blemish.

According to Ephesians 5:26, Christ gave Himself up for the
church so that "He might sanctify her, cleansing her by the washing of the water in the word." After the Lord Jesus gave Himself
for us in the flesh, He was resurrected and in resurrection became
the life-giving Spirit (1 Cor. 15:45). As the life-giving Spirit, He is
the speaking Spirit. Whatever He speaks is the word that washes
us. The Greek word rendered word in verse 26 is not *logos,* the
constant word, but *rhema,* which denotes the instant word, the
word the Lord presently speaks to us. As the life-giving Spirit, the
Lord is not silent; He is constantly speaking. If you take Him as
your person, you will discover how much He desires to speak
within you. Idols are dumb, but the indwelling Christ is always
speaking. No one who takes Christ as his life and his person can
remain silent. On the contrary, he will be constrained by Christ to
speak. (*Life-study of Ephesians,* p. 465)

Today's Reading

In John 6:63 the Lord Jesus said, "The words which I have spoken to you are spirit and are life." The Greek word rendered words
here is also *rhema,* the instant and present spoken word.... As the
speaking Spirit, the Lord is speaking the *rhema* to us. Whatever
He speaks is spirit.

If day by day there is no speaking of the Lord within us, it is an
indication that there is some problem within us....Then in our
practical experience the Spirit is absent, for the Lord's speaking
actually is the Spirit. As long as we have the Lord's present word,
we have the Spirit, the life-giving Spirit. We cannot separate
Christ as the life-giving Spirit from His speaking. His presence

consists in His speaking....If we do not have His speaking within us, we do not have His presence. But if we turn to Him, to mean business to take Christ as our life and our person, His speaking will begin again. His speaking is the living word,...the Spirit, and ...our wonderful Christ Himself. How practical, subjective, intimate, and real He is as the speaking Spirit!

This Spirit is the water that washes us. The more the Spirit speaks, the more we are washed, cleansed....This cleansing is a metabolic cleansing that removes what is old and replaces it with what is new....By the metabolic cleansing that comes from the speaking of Christ as the life-giving Spirit, we are truly changed, transformed.

Because such an inward transformation is taking place within us, there is no need for outward correction in the church life. God's way in His economy is not to change us outwardly. His way is for Christ to give Himself up for us and then to come into us as the life-giving Spirit....[The] speaking of the life-giving Spirit within is the water that cleanses our inner being. This cleansing water deposits a new element into us to replace the old element in our nature and disposition,...caus[ing] a genuine change in life....Outward correction has no value. What the church needs is the inward metabolic cleansing that comes from allowing Christ as the life-giving Spirit to be our life and our person.

Through the Lord's speaking within us as the life-giving Spirit, we are becoming a glorious church, a church holy and without blemish. Today we are waiting for the Lord's coming back, knowing that when He comes, He will present us to Himself a glorious church, holy and without blemish. At that time, we shall experience Christ...as the Bridegroom coming for His bride. Until then, our need is to daily take Christ as our person and to be cleansed, purified, and sanctified, through the speaking of the life-giving Spirit. In this way we shall undergo a metabolic change leading to the transformation in life which is necessary for the church life. (*Life-study of Ephesians,* pp. 465-467, 469)

Further Reading: Life-study of Ephesians, msgs. 55-57, 71

Enlightenment and inspiration: _____
_____
_____
_____

Morning Nourishment

Eph. **And receive the helmet of salvation and the sword**
6:17-18 **of the Spirit, which *Spirit* is the word of God, by**
means of all prayer and petition, praying at every
time in spirit and watching unto this in all perse-
verance and petition concerning all the saints.

Pray-reading is a practical way to kill the negative elements within us. The more we take the word of God by means of all prayer in spirit, the more the negative things within us will be put to death. Thus, pray-reading is not only feasting; it is also a way of fighting. As we pray-read the word, the battle is raging as the negative elements in our being are slain. Eventually, the self, the worst foe of all, will be put to death. When the negative things in us are killed through pray-reading, the Lord is victorious. Because He is victorious, we are victorious also.

Pray-reading is the way to kill the adversary within us. Every day and in every kind of situation, you should pray-read. Whenever you are troubled by something negative within you, take the word of God by means of prayer in spirit. As you do this, the negative element will be killed.

In Ephesians 5 the word is for nourishment that leads to the beautifying of the Bride. But in Ephesians 6 the word is for killing that enables the church as the corporate warrior to engage in spiritual warfare. Through the killing word, the adversary within us is slain. Sometimes we gain the victory over the enemy objectively, but we are defeated by the adversary subjectively. Although we may rejoice that the enemy outwardly is fleeing, we are still troubled by the adversary within us who remains. For this reason, we should be more concerned for the hidden adversary within us. Let us kill the adversary by pray-reading the word. (*Life-study of Ephesians*, pp. 821-822)

Today's Reading

Let us now turn to Ephesians 6:17. Here Paul charges us to receive "the sword of the Spirit, which Spirit is the word of God." When I was a young Christian, I did not understand how the word of God could be a sword. I understood what it means to be enlightened by the Bible, for by reading the Bible I was enlightened. To some extent, by the Bible I was also rebuked, corrected, and instructed to be right with God and man. But I did not know how the Bible could become a sword, an offensive weapon to deal with the enemy. To understand this requires spiritual experience.

It is common for Christians to be enlightened, rebuked, corrected, and instructed by the Bible, but not many experience the word of the Bible as a sword that kills the enemy. The reason for this lack of experience is that we may receive the word of the Bible for teaching, rebuke, correction, and instruction without touching the Spirit. Even unbelievers may be enlightened by what they read in the Scriptures. Also, they may be rebuked, corrected, and instructed by what the Bible says concerning honor, love, humility, and honesty. However, in their reading of the Scriptures there is nothing of the Spirit. However, if we would take the word of the Bible as a sword for fighting the enemy, we must touch the Bible in a way that is full of the Spirit.

According to Paul's word in Ephesians 6:17, the word of God is the sword not directly but indirectly. Paul speaks of "the sword of the Spirit, which Spirit is the word of God." Here we have indirectness. The sword is not the word directly. Rather, the sword is the Spirit directly, and then the Spirit is the word. This indicates that if we would deal with the enemy Satan, the Bible must become the Spirit. Without the Spirit it may be possible for us to teach from the Bible that the young people should honor their parents and ask for forgiveness for what they have done wrong. But if we would use the word of the Bible as a sword to kill the enemy, in our experience the word must be the Spirit. (*Teachers' Training,* pp. 20-21)

Further Reading: The Divine Spirit with the Human Spirit in the Epistles, ch. 7; *Life-study of Ephesians,* msg. 97

Enlightenment and inspiration: _____

_____

_____

Morning Nourishment

Eph.   For our wrestling is not against blood and flesh but
6:12-13 against the rulers, against the authorities, against
the world-rulers of this darkness, against the spiritual *forces* of evil in the heavenlies. Therefore take
up the whole armor of God...

17-18 And receive the helmet of salvation and the sword
of the Spirit, which *Spirit* is the word of God, by
means of all prayer and petition...

Ephesians 6:12 reveals that our enemies are the evil spirits,
"the world-rulers of this darkness," "the spiritual forces of evil in
the heavenlies."...Ephesians, a book on the church as the Body of
Christ, talks about the Body life, the oneness of the Body (4:4),
and the Body being the fullness of the One who fills all in all
(1:23). We need to realize that things such as our opinion, thought,
temper, emotion, natural life, and point of view are often used by
the powers of darkness in the air to damage the Body life. As
brothers and sisters in the church, we all have our emotion,
thought, opinion, and natural life, and we all have our own point
of view. Quite often we are offended, not due to the wrongdoings of
others but simply due to our emotion or opinion.....It is easy for
brothers and sisters in the church to be offended.

Suppose an older brother speaks a word to a particular sister
and she is offended because of her emotion. Then the evil power in
the air comes in to take advantage of her emotion, and she deter-
mines not to forget that she has been offended. Apparently the
problem is her emotion. Actually the problem is that her emotion
has been taken over by the evil force in the air....The real enemy
is not this sister's emotion but the evil spirit in the air that takes
advantage of her emotion in order to damage the church life.
Because of the enemy's use of her emotion, this sister first has
a negative effect on her husband, and then she goes on to have a
negative effect on several others. As a result, part of the Body is
poisoned. If the enemy is to be defeated in this situation, the sister
must learn to receive the word as the Spirit, which becomes the
sword to deal with the enemy. (*Teachers' Training*, pp. 21-22)

Today's Reading

I have learned through many years of experience...[that] the word I receive as the Spirit...becomes the sword to slay the enemy. Apparently the sword of the Spirit kills my emotion; actually it kills the evil spirit in the air who takes advantage of my emotion. Whereas my emotion is killed directly, the evil spirit is killed indirectly. In this way I have been able to get through the offenses.

Without the word as the Spirit to be the killing sword, there would be no way for us to be kept in the church life over the years....We may compare this kind of killing to the effect of an antibiotic on the germs that cause illness in our body. In order for our body to be saved, the germs need to be killed by an antibiotic. The word that we receive in a living way as the Spirit is a spiritual antibiotic that kills the "germs" within us. When the germs are killed, the evil forces in the air have no way to take advantage of us. Then we can live a healthy Body life, a healthy church life.

This is the way I have been preserved in the church life and in my ministry for so many years. Apart from the killing through the word as the Spirit, my ministry would have been terminated. Once again I would emphasize that we need to receive the word of God in a living way, so that in our experience the Spirit becomes the killing sword. When the word becomes the Spirit, the Spirit becomes the sword—the sword of the Spirit that kills the germs in us and the evil spirits in the air. In this way the Body, the church life, and our ministry are saved. This will enable our ministry to have a long life. However, the ministry of certain brothers has not lasted long. In their situation it was their ministry and not the enemy that was killed.

Let us all receive the word of God in a living way! As long as in our experience the word becomes the Spirit, the word will not only heal us but also kill the enemy. (*Teachers' Training*, pp. 22-24)

Further Reading: Teachers' Training, ch. 2

Enlightenment and inspiration: _____

_____

_____

_____

Hymns, #837

1   We praise Thee, Lord, for Thy great plan
That we Thy dwelling-place may be;
Thou live in us, we filled with Thee,
Thou in the Son expressed might be.

2   Though in Thine image made by Thee
And given Thine authority,
Yet we are only made of clay
Without a trace of divinity.

3   When we receive Thee as our life,
Thy nature we thru grace possess;
Mingled together, we with Thee
One Body glorious will express.

4   When flows Thy life thru all our souls,
Filling, renewing every part,
We will be pearls and precious stones,
Changed to Thine image, as Thou art.

5   But, Lord, we fully realize
These are not wrought men's praise to rouse,
But as material to be built
Together for Thy glorious house.

6   Here, Lord, we give ourselves to Thee;
Receive us into Thy wise hands;
Bend, break, and build together in Thee
To be the house to meet Thy demands.

7   Break all the natural life for us,
Deal Thou with each peculiar way,
That we no more independent be
But with all saints are one for aye.

8   Then we shall be Thy Bride beloved,
Together in Thy chamber abide,
Enjoy the fulness of Thy love.
How Thou wilt then be satisfied!

Composition for prophecy with main point and sub-points: _____

_____
_____
_____
_____
_____
_____
_____
_____
_____
_____
_____
_____
_____
_____
_____
_____
_____
_____
_____
_____
_____
_____
_____
_____
_____
_____
_____
_____
_____
_____
_____
_____
_____
_____
_____
_____
_____
_____
_____
_____
_____
_____

Reading Schedule for the Recovery Version of the Old Testament with Footnotes

Wk.	Lord's Day	Monday	Tuesday	Wednesday	Thursday	Friday	Saturday
1	Gen 1:1-5	1:6-23	1:24-31	2:1-9	2:10-25	3:1-13	3:14-24
2	4:1-26	5:1-32	6:1-22	7:1—8:3	8:4-22	9:1-29	10:1-32
3	11:1-32	12:1-20	13:1-18	14:1-24	15:1-21	16:1-16	17:1-27
4	18:1-33	19:1-38	20:1-18	21:1-34	22:1-24	23:1—24:27	24:28-67
5	25:1-34	26:1-35	27:1-46	28:1-22	29:1-35	30:1-43	31:1-55
6	32:1-32	33:1—34:31	35:1-29	36:1-43	37:1-36	38:1—39:23	40:1—41:13
7	41:14-57	42:1-38	43:1-34	44:1-34	45:1-28	46:1-34	47:1-31
8	48:1-22	49:1-15	49:16-33	50:1-26	Exo 1:1-22	2:1-25	3:1-22
9	4:1-31	5:1-23	6:1-30	7:1-25	8:1-32	9:1-35	10:1-29
10	11:1-10	12:1-14	12:15-36	12:37-51	13:1-22	14:1-31	15:1-27
11	16:1-36	17:1-16	18:1-27	19:1-25	20:1-26	21:1-36	22:1-31
12	23:1-33	24:1-18	25:1-22	25:23-40	26:1-14	26:15-37	27:1-21
13	28:1-21	28:22-43	29:1-21	29:22-46	30:1-10	30:11-38	31:1-17
14	31:18—32:35	33:1-23	34:1-35	35:1-35	36:1-38	37:1-29	38:1-31
15	39:1-43	40:1-38	Lev 1:1-17	2:1-16	3:1-17	4:1-35	5:1-19
16	6:1-30	7:1-38	8:1-36	9:1-24	10:1-20	11:1-47	12:1-8
17	13:1-28	13:29-59	14:1-18	14:19-32	14:33-57	15:1-33	16:1-17
18	16:18-34	17:1-16	18:1-30	19:1-37	20:1-27	21:1-24	22:1-33
19	23:1-22	23:23-44	24:1-23	25:1-23	25:24-55	26:1-24	26:25-46
20	27:1-34	Num 1:1-54	2:1-34	3:1-51	4:1-49	5:1-31	6:1-27
21	7:1-41	7:42-88	7:89—8:26	9:1-23	10:1-36	11:1-35	12:1—13:33
22	14:1-45	15:1-41	16:1-50	17:1—18:7	18:8-32	19:1-22	20:1-29
23	21:1-35	22:1-41	23:1-30	24:1-25	25:1-18	26:1-65	27:1-23
24	28:1-31	29:1-40	30:1—31:24	31:25-54	32:1-42	33:1-56	34:1-29
25	35:1-34	36:1-13	Deut 1:1-46	2:1-37	3:1-29	4:1-49	5:1-33
26	6:1—7:26	8:1-20	9:1-29	10:1-22	11:1-32	12:1-32	13:1—14:21

Reading Schedule for the Recovery Version of the Old Testament with Footnotes

Wk.	Lord's Day	Monday	Tuesday	Wednesday	Thursday	Friday	Saturday
27	☐ 14:22—15:23	☐ 16:1-22	☐ 17:1—18:8	☐ 18:9—19:21	☐ 20:1—21:17	☐ 21:18—22:30	☐ 23:1-25
28	☐ 24:1-22	☐ 25:1-19	☐ 26:1-19	☐ 27:1-26	☐ 28:1-68	☐ 29:1-29	☐ 30:1—31:29
29	☐ 31:30—32:52	☐ 33:1-29	☐ 34:1-12	☐ Josh 1:1-18	☐ 2:1-24	☐ 3:1-17	☐ 4:1-24
30	☐ 5:1-15	☐ 6:1-27	☐ 7:1-26	☐ 8:1-35	☐ 9:1-27	☐ 10:1-43	☐ 11:1—12:24
31	☐ 13:1-33	☐ 14:1—15:63	☐ 16:1—18:28	☐ 19:1-51	☐ 20:1—21:45	☐ 22:1-34	☐ 23:1—24:33
32	☐ Judg 1:1-36	☐ 2:1-23	☐ 3:1-31	☐ 4:1-24	☐ 5:1-31	☐ 6:1-40	☐ 7:1-25
33	☐ 8:1-35	☐ 9:1-57	☐ 10:1—11:40	☐ 12:1—13:25	☐ 14:1—15:20	☐ 16:1-31	☐ 17:1—18:31
34	☐ 19:1-30	☐ 20:1-48	☐ 21:1-25	☐ Ruth 1:1-22	☐ 2:1-23	☐ 3:1-18	☐ 4:1-22
35	☐ 1 Sam 1:1-28	☐ 2:1-36	☐ 3:1—4:22	☐ 5:1—6:21	☐ 7:1—8:22	☐ 9:1-27	☐ 10:1—11:15
36	☐ 12:1—13:23	☐ 14:1-52	☐ 15:1-35	☐ 16:1-23	☐ 17:1-58	☐ 18:1-30	☐ 19:1-24
37	☐ 20:1-42	☐ 21:1—22:23	☐ 23:1—24:22	☐ 25:1-44	☐ 26:1-25	☐ 27:1—28:25	☐ 29:1—30:31
38	☐ 31:1-13	☐ 2 Sam 1:1-27	☐ 2:1-32	☐ 3:1-39	☐ 4:1—5:25	☐ 6:1-23	☐ 7:1-29
39	☐ 8:1—9:13	☐ 10:1—11:27	☐ 12:1-31	☐ 13:1-39	☐ 14:1-33	☐ 15:1—16:23	☐ 17:1—18:33
40	☐ 19:1-43	☐ 20:1—21:22	☐ 22:1-51	☐ 23:1-39	☐ 24:1-25	☐ 1 Kings 1:1-19	☐ 1:20-53
41	☐ 2:1-46	☐ 3:1-28	☐ 4:1-34	☐ 5:1—6:38	☐ 7:1-22	☐ 7:23-51	☐ 8:1-36
42	☐ 8:37-66	☐ 9:1-28	☐ 10:1-29	☐ 11:1-43	☐ 12:1-33	☐ 13:1-34	☐ 14:1-31
43	☐ 15:1-34	☐ 16:1—17:24	☐ 18:1-46	☐ 19:1-21	☐ 20:1-43	☐ 21:1—22:53	☐ 2 Kings 1:1-18
44	☐ 2:1—3:27	☐ 4:1-44	☐ 5:1—6:33	☐ 7:1-20	☐ 8:1-29	☐ 9:1-37	☐ 10:1-36
45	☐ 11:1—12:21	☐ 13:1—14:29	☐ 15:1-38	☐ 16:1-20	☐ 17:1-41	☐ 18:1-37	☐ 19:1-37
46	☐ 20:1—21:26	☐ 22:1-20	☐ 23:1-37	☐ 24:1—25:30	☐ 1 Chron 1:1-54	☐ 2:1—3:24	☐ 4:1—5:26
47	☐ 6:1-81	☐ 7:1-40	☐ 8:1-40	☐ 9:1-44	☐ 10:1—11:47	☐ 12:1-40	☐ 13:1—14:17
48	☐ 15:1—16:43	☐ 17:1-27	☐ 18:1—19:19	☐ 20:1—21:30	☐ 22:1—23:32	☐ 24:1—25:31	☐ 26:1-32
49	☐ 27:1-34	☐ 28:1—29:30	☐ 2 Chron 1:1-17	☐ 2:1—3:17	☐ 4:1—5:14	☐ 6:1-42	☐ 7:1—8:18
50	☐ 9:1—10:19	☐ 11:1—12:16	☐ 13:1—15:19	☐ 16:1—17:19	☐ 18:1—19:11	☐ 20:1-37	☐ 21:1—22:12
51	☐ 23:1—24:27	☐ 25:1—26:23	☐ 27:1—28:27	☐ 29:1-36	☐ 30:1—31:21	☐ 32:1-33	☐ 33:1—34:33
52	☐ 35:1—36:23	☐ Ezra 1:1-11	☐ 2:1-70	☐ 3:1—4:24	☐ 5:1—6:22	☐ 7:1-28	☐ 8:1-36

Reading Schedule for the Recovery Version of the Old Testament with Footnotes

Wk.	Lord's Day	Monday	Tuesday	Wednesday	Thursday	Friday	Saturday
53	☐ 9:1—10:44	☐ Neh 1:1-11	☐ 2:1—3:32	☐ 4:1—5:19	☐ 6:1-19	☐ 7:1-73	☐ 8:1-18
54	☐ 9:1-20	☐ 9:21-38	☐ 10:1—11:36	☐ 12:1-47	☐ 13:1-31	☐ Esth 1:1-22	☐ 2:1—3:15
55	☐ 4:1—5:14	☐ 6:1—7:10	☐ 8:1-17	☐ 9:1—10:3	☐ Job 1:1-22	☐ 2:1—3:26	☐ 4:1—5:27
56	☐ 6:1—7:21	☐ 8:1—9:35	☐ 10:1—11:20	☐ 12:1—13:28	☐ 14:1—15:35	☐ 16:1—17:16	☐ 18:1—19:29
57	☐ 20:1—21:34	☐ 22:1—23:17	☐ 24:1—25:6	☐ 26:1—27:23	☐ 28:1—29:25	☐ 30:1—31:40	☐ 32:1—33:33
58	☐ 34:1—35:16	☐ 36:1-33	☐ 37:1-24	☐ 38:1-41	☐ 39:1-30	☐ 40:1-24	☐ 41:1-34
59	☐ 42:1-17	☐ Psa 1:1-6	☐ 2:1—3:8	☐ 4:1—6:10	☐ 7:1—8:9	☐ 9:1—10:18	☐ 11:1—15:5
60	☐ 16:1—17:15	☐ 18:1-50	☐ 19:1—21:13	☐ 22:1-31	☐ 23:1—24:10	☐ 25:1—27:14	☐ 28:1—30:12
61	☐ 31:1—32:11	☐ 33:1—34:22	☐ 35:1—36:12	☐ 37:1-40	☐ 38:1—39:13	☐ 40:1—41:13	☐ 42:1—43:5
62	☐ 44:1-26	☐ 45:1-17	☐ 46:1—48:14	☐ 49:1—50:23	☐ 51:1—52:9	☐ 53:1—55:23	☐ 56:1—58:11
63	☐ 59:1—61:8	☐ 62:1—64:10	☐ 65:1—67:7	☐ 68:1-35	☐ 69:1—70:5	☐ 71:1—72:20	☐ 73:1—74:23
64	☐ 75:1—77:20	☐ 78:1-72	☐ 79:1—81:16	☐ 82:1—84:12	☐ 85:1—87:7	☐ 88:1—89:52	☐ 90:1—91:16
65	☐ 92:1—94:23	☐ 95:1—97:12	☐ 98:1—101:8	☐ 102:1—103:22	☐ 104:1—105:45	☐ 106:1-48	☐ 107:1-43
66	☐ 108:1—109:31	☐ 110:1—112:10	☐ 113:1—115:18	☐ 116:1—118:29	☐ 119:1-32	☐ 119:33-72	☐ 119:73-120
67	☐ 119:121-176	☐ 120:1—124:8	☐ 125:1—128:6	☐ 129:1—132:18	☐ 133:1—135:21	☐ 136:1—138:8	☐ 139:1—140:13
68	☐ 141:1—144:15	☐ 145:1—147:20	☐ 148:1—150:6	☐ Prov 1:1-33	☐ 2:1—3:35	☐ 4:1—5:23	☐ 6:1-35
69	☐ 7:1—8:36	☐ 9:1—10:32	☐ 11:1—12:28	☐ 13:1—14:35	☐ 15:1-33	☐ 16:1-33	☐ 17:1-28
70	☐ 18:1-24	☐ 19:1—20:30	☐ 21:1—22:29	☐ 23:1-35	☐ 24:1—25:28	☐ 26:1—27:27	☐ 28:1—29:27
71	☐ 30:1-33	☐ 31:1-31	☐ Eccl 1:1-18	☐ 2:1—3:22	☐ 4:1—5:20	☐ 6:1—7:29	☐ 8:1—9:18
72	☐ 10:1—11:10	☐ 12:1-14	☐ S.S 1:1-8	☐ 1:9-17	☐ 2:1-17	☐ 3:1-11	☐ 4:1-8
73	☐ 4:9-16	☐ 5:1-16	☐ 6:1-13	☐ 7:1-13	☐ 8:1-14	☐ Isa 1:1-11	☐ 1:12-31
74	☐ 2:1-22	☐ 3:1-26	☐ 4:1-6	☐ 5:1-30	☐ 6:1-13	☐ 7:1-25	☐ 8:1-22
75	☐ 9:1-21	☐ 10:1-34	☐ 11:1—12:6	☐ 13:1-22	☐ 14:1-14	☐ 14:15-32	☐ 15:1—16:14
76	☐ 17:1—18:7	☐ 19:1-25	☐ 20:1—21:17	☐ 22:1-25	☐ 23:1-18	☐ 24:1-23	☐ 25:1-12
77	☐ 26:1-21	☐ 27:1-13	☐ 28:1-29	☐ 29:1-24	☐ 30:1-33	☐ 31:1—32:20	☐ 33:1-24
78	☐ 34:1-17	☐ 35:1-10	☐ 36:1-22	☐ 37:1-38	☐ 38:1—39:8	☐ 40:1-31	☐ 41:1-29

Reading Schedule for the Recovery Version of the Old Testament with Footnotes

Wk.	Lord's Day	Monday	Tuesday	Wednesday	Thursday	Friday	Saturday
79	☐ 42:1-25	☐ 43:1-28	☐ 44:1-28	☐ 45:1-25	☐ 46:1-13	☐ 47:1-15	☐ 48:1-22
80	☐ 49:1-13	☐ 49:14-26	☐ 50:1—51:23	☐ 52:1-15	☐ 53:1-12	☐ 54:1-17	☐ 55:1-13
81	☐ 56:1-12	☐ 57:1-21	☐ 58:1-14	☐ 59:1-21	☐ 60:1-22	☐ 61:1-11	☐ 62:1-12
82	☐ 63:1-19	☐ 64:1-12	☐ 65:1-25	☐ 66:1-24	☐ Jer 1:1-19	☐ 2:1-19	☐ 2:20-37
83	☐ 3:1-25	☐ 4:1-31	☐ 5:1-31	☐ 6:1-30	☐ 7:1-34	☐ 8:1-22	☐ 9:1-26
84	☐ 10:1-25	☐ 11:1—12:17	☐ 13:1-27	☐ 14:1-22	☐ 15:1-21	☐ 16:1—17:27	☐ 18:1-23
85	☐ 19:1—20:18	☐ 21:1—22:30	☐ 23:1-40	☐ 24:1—25:38	☐ 26:1—27:22	☐ 28:1—29:32	☐ 30:1-24
86	☐ 31:1-23	☐ 31:24-40	☐ 32:1-44	☐ 33:1-26	☐ 34:1-22	☐ 35:1-19	☐ 36:1-32
87	☐ 37:1-21	☐ 38:1-28	☐ 39:1—40:16	☐ 41:1—42:22	☐ 43:1—44:30	☐ 45:1—46:28	☐ 47:1—48:16
88	☐ 48:17-47	☐ 49:1-22	☐ 49:23-39	☐ 50:1-27	☐ 50:28-46	☐ 51:1-27	☐ 51:28-64
89	☐ 52:1-34	☐ Lam 1:1-22	☐ 2:1-22	☐ 3:1-39	☐ 3:40-66	☐ 4:1-22	☐ 5:1-22
90	☐ Ezek 1:1-14	☐ 1:15-28	☐ 2:1—3:27	☐ 4:1—5:17	☐ 6:1—7:27	☐ 8:1—9:11	☐ 10:1—11:25
91	☐ 12:1—13:23	☐ 14:1—15:8	☐ 16:1-63	☐ 17:1—18:32	☐ 19:1-14	☐ 20:1-49	☐ 21:1-32
92	☐ 22:1-31	☐ 23:1-49	☐ 24:1-27	☐ 25:1—26:21	☐ 27:1-36	☐ 28:1-26	☐ 29:1—30:26
93	☐ 31:1—32:32	☐ 33:1-33	☐ 34:1-31	☐ 35:1—36:21	☐ 36:22-38	☐ 37:1-28	☐ 38:1—39:29
94	☐ 40:1-27	☐ 40:28-49	☐ 41:1-26	☐ 42:1—43:27	☐ 44:1-31	☐ 45:1-25	☐ 46:1-24
95	☐ 47:1-23	☐ 48:1-35	☐ Dan 1:1-21	☐ 2:1-30	☐ 2:31-49	☐ 3:1-30	☐ 4:1-37
96	☐ 5:1-31	☐ 6:1-28	☐ 7:1-12	☐ 7:13-28	☐ 8:1-27	☐ 9:1-27	☐ 10:1-21
97	☐ 11:1-22	☐ 11:23-45	☐ 12:1-13	☐ Hosea 1:1-11	☐ 2:1-23	☐ 3:1—4:19	☐ 5:1-15
98	☐ 6:1-11	☐ 7:1-16	☐ 8:1-14	☐ 9:1-17	☐ 10:1-15	☐ 11:1-12	☐ 12:1-14
99	☐ 13:1—14:9	☐ Joel 1:1-20	☐ 2:1-16	☐ 2:17-32	☐ 3:1-21	☐ Amos 1:1-15	☐ 2:1-16
100	☐ 3:1-15	☐ 4:1—5:27	☐ 6:1—7:17	☐ 8:1—9:15	☐ Obad 1-21	☐ Jonah 1:1-17	☐ 2:1—4:11
101	☐ Micah 1:1-16	☐ 2:1—3:12	☐ 4:1—5:15	☐ 6:1—7:20	☐ Nahum 1:1-15	☐ 2:1—3:19	☐ Hab 1:1-17
102	☐ 2:1-20	☐ 3:1-19	☐ Zeph 1:1-18	☐ 2:1-15	☐ 3:1-20	☐ Hag 1:1-15	☐ 2:1-23
103	☐ Zech 1:1-21	☐ 2:1-13	☐ 3:1-10	☐ 4:1-14	☐ 5:1—6:15	☐ 7:1—8:23	☐ 9:1-17
104	☐ 10:1—11:17	☐ 12:1—13:9	☐ 14:1-21	☐ Mal 1:1-14	☐ 2:1-17	☐ 3:1-18	☐ 4:1-6

Reading Schedule for the Recovery Version of the New Testament with Footnotes

Wk.	Lord's Day	Monday	Tuesday	Wednesday	Thursday	Friday	Saturday
1	Matt 1:1-2	1:3-7	1:8-17	1:18-25	2:1-23	3:1-6	3:7-17
2	4:1-11	4:12-25	5:1-4	5:5-12	5:13-20	5:21-26	5:27-48
3	6:1-8	6:9-18	6:19-34	7:1-12	7:13-29	8:1-13	8:14-22
4	8:23-34	9:1-13	9:14-17	9:18-34	9:35—10:5	10:6-25	10:26-42
5	11:1-15	11:16-30	12:1-14	12:15-32	12:33-42	12:43—13:2	13:3-12
6	13:13-30	13:31-43	13:44-58	14:1-13	14:14-21	14:22-36	15:1-20
7	15:21-31	15:32-39	16:1-12	16:13-20	16:21-28	17:1-13	17:14-27
8	18:1-14	18:15-22	18:23-35	19:1-15	19:16-30	20:1-16	20:17-34
9	21:1-11	21:12-22	21:23-32	21:33-46	22:1-22	22:23-33	22:34-46
10	23:1-12	23:13-39	24:1-14	24:15-31	24:32-51	25:1-13	25:14-30
11	25:31-46	26:1-16	26:17-35	26:36-46	26:47-64	26:65-75	27:1-26
12	27:27-44	27:45-56	27:57—28:15	28:16-20	Mark 1:1	1:2-6	1:7-13
13	1:14-28	1:29-45	2:1-12	2:13-28	3:1-19	3:20-35	4:1-25
14	4:26-41	5:1-20	5:21-43	6:1-29	6:30-56	7:1-23	7:24-37
15	8:1-26	8:27—9:1	9:2-29	9:30-50	10:1-16	10:17-34	10:35-52
16	11:1-16	11:17-33	12:1-27	12:28-44	13:1-13	13:14-37	14:1-26
17	14:27-52	14:53-72	15:1-15	15:16-47	16:1-8	16:9-20	Luke 1:1-4
18	1:5-25	1:26-46	1:47-56	1:57-80	2:1-8	2:9-20	2:21-39
19	2:40-52	3:1-20	3:21-38	4:1-13	4:14-30	4:31-44	5:1-26
20	5:27—6:16	6:17-38	6:39-49	7:1-17	7:18-23	7:24-35	7:36-50
21	8:1-15	8:16-25	8:26-39	8:40-56	9:1-17	9:18-26	9:27-36
22	9:37-50	9:51-62	10:1-11	10:12-24	10:25-37	10:38-42	11:1-13
23	11:14-26	11:27-36	11:37-54	12:1-12	12:13-21	12:22-34	12:35-48
24	12:49-59	13:1-9	13:10-17	13:18-30	13:31—14:6	14:7-14	14:15-24
25	14:25-35	15:1-10	15:11-21	15:22-32	16:1-13	16:14-22	16:23-31
26	17:1-19	17:20-37	18:1-14	18:15-30	18:31-43	19:1-10	19:11-27

Reading Schedule for the Recovery Version of the New Testament with Footnotes

Wk.	Lord's Day	Monday	Tuesday	Wednesday	Thursday	Friday	Saturday
27	Luke 19:28-48	20:1-19	20:20-38	20:39—21:4	21:5-27	21:28-38	22:1-20
28	22:21-38	22:39-54	22:55-71	23:1-43	23:44-56	24:1-12	24:13-35
29	24:36-53	John 1:1-13	1:14-18	1:19-34	1:35-51	2:1-11	2:12-22
30	2:23—3:13	3:14-21	3:22-36	4:1-14	4:15-26	4:27-42	4:43-54
31	5:1-16	5:17-30	5:31-47	6:1-15	6:16-31	6:32-51	6:52-71
32	7:1-9	7:10-24	7:25-36	7:37-52	7:53—8:11	8:12-27	8:28-44
33	8:45-59	9:1-13	9:14-34	9:35—10:9	10:10-30	10:31—11:4	11:5-22
34	11:23-40	11:41-57	12:1-11	12:12-24	12:25-36	12:37-50	13:1-11
35	13:12-30	13:31-38	14:1-6	14:7-20	14:21-31	15:1-11	15:12-27
36	16:1-15	16:16-33	17:1-5	17:6-13	17:14-24	17:25—18:11	18:12-27
37	18:28-40	19:1-16	19:17-30	19:31-42	20:1-13	20:14-18	20:19-22
38	20:23-31	21:1-14	21:15-22	21:23-25	Acts 1:1-8	1:9-14	1:15-26
39	2:1-13	2:14-21	2:22-36	2:37-41	2:42-47	3:1-18	3:19—4:22
40	4:23-37	5:1-16	5:17-32	5:33-42	6:1—7:1	7:2-29	7:30-60
41	8:1-13	8:14-25	8:26-40	9:1-19	9:20-43	10:1-16	10:17-33
42	10:34-48	11:1-18	11:19-30	12:1-25	13:1-12	13:13-43	13:44—14:5
43	14:6-28	15:1-12	15:13-34	15:35—16:5	16:6-18	16:19-40	17:1-18
44	17:19-34	18:1-17	18:18-28	19:1-20	19:21-41	20:1-12	20:13-38
45	21:1-14	21:15-26	21:27-40	22:1-21	22:22-29	22:30—23:11	23:12-15
46	23:16-30	23:31—24:21	24:22—25:5	25:6-27	26:1-13	26:14-32	27:1-26
47	27:27—28:10	28:11-22	28:23-31	Rom 1:1-2	1:3-7	1:8-17	1:18-25
48	1:26—2:10	2:11-29	3:1-20	3:21-31	4:1-12	4:13-25	5:1-11
49	5:12-17	5:18—6:5	6:6-11	6:12-23	7:1-12	7:13-25	8:1-2
50	8:3-6	8:7-13	8:14-25	8:26-39	9:1-18	9:19—10:3	10:4-15
51	10:16—11:10	11:11-22	11:23-36	12:1-3	12:4-21	13:1-14	14:1-12
52	14:13-23	15:1-13	15:14-33	16:1-5	16:6-24	16:25-27	1 Cor 1:1-4

Reading Schedule for the Recovery Version of the New Testament with Footnotes

Wk.	Lord's Day	Monday	Tuesday	Wednesday	Thursday	Friday	Saturday
53	1 Cor 1:5-9	1:10-17	1:18-31	2:1-5	2:6-10	2:11-16	3:1-9
54	3:10-13	3:14-23	4:1-9	4:10-21	5:1-13	6:1-11	6:12-20
55	7:1-16	7:17-24	7:25-40	8:1-13	9:1-15	9:16-27	10:1-4
56	10:5-13	10:14-33	11:1-6	11:7-16	11:17-26	11:27-34	12:1-11
57	12:12-22	12:23-31	13:1-13	14:1-12	14:13-25	14:26-33	14:34-40
58	15:1-19	15:20-28	15:29-34	15:35-49	15:50-58	16:1-9	16:10-24
59	2 Cor 1:1-4	1:5-14	1:15-22	1:23—2:11	2:12-17	3:1-6	3:7-11
60	3:12-18	4:1-6	4:7-12	4:13-18	5:1-8	5:9-15	5:16-21
61	6:1-13	6:14—7:4	7:5-16	8:1-15	8:16-24	9:1-15	10:1-6
62	10:7-18	11:1-15	11:16-33	12:1-10	12:11-21	13:1-10	13:11-14
63	Gal 1:1-5	1:6-14	1:15-24	2:1-13	2:14-21	3:1-4	3:5-14
64	3:15-22	3:23-29	4:1-7	4:8-20	4:21-31	5:1-12	5:13-21
65	5:22-26	6:1-10	6:11-15	6:16-18	Eph 1:1-3	1:4-6	1:7-10
66	1:11-14	1:15-18	1:19-23	2:1-5	2:6-10	2:11-14	2:15-18
67	2:19-22	3:1-7	3:8-13	3:14-18	3:19-21	4:1-4	4:5-10
68	4:11-16	4:17-24	4:25-32	5:1-10	5:11-21	5:22-26	5:27-33
69	6:1-9	6:10-14	6:15-18	6:19-24	Phil 1:1-7	1:8-18	1:19-26
70	1:27—2:4	2:5-11	2:12-16	2:17-30	3:1-6	3:7-11	3:12-16
71	3:17-21	4:1-9	4:10-23	Col 1:1-8	1:9-13	1:14-23	1:24-29
72	2:1-7	2:8-15	2:16-23	3:1-4	3:5-15	3:16-25	4:1-18
73	1 Thes 1:1-3	1:4-10	2:1-12	2:13—3:5	3:6-13	4:1-10	4:11—5:11
74	5:12-28	2 Thes 1:1-12	2:1-17	3:1-18	1 Tim 1:1-2	1:3-4	1:5-14
75	1:15-20	2:1-7	2:8-15	3:1-13	3:14—4:5	4:6-16	5:1-25
76	6:1-10	6:11-21	2 Tim 1:1-10	1:11-18	2:1-15	2:16-26	3:1-13
77	3:14—4:8	4:9-22	Titus 1:1-4	1:5-16	2:1-15	3:1-8	3:9-15
78	Philem 1:1-11	1:12-25	Heb 1:1-2	1:3-5	1:6-14	2:1-9	2:10-18

Reading Schedule for the Recovery Version of the New Testament with Footnotes

Wk.	Lord's Day	Monday	Tuesday	Wednesday	Thursday	Friday	Saturday
79	Heb 3:1-6	3:7-19	4:1-9	4:10-13	4:14-16	5:1-10	5:11—6:3
80	6:4-8	6:9-20	7:1-10	7:11-28	8:1-6	8:7-13	9:1-4
81	9:5-14	9:15-28	10:1-18	10:19-28	10:29-39	11:1-6	11:7-19
82	11:20-31	11:32-40	12:1-2	12:3-13	12:14-17	12:18-26	12:27-29
83	13:1-7	13:8-12	13:13-15	13:16-25	James 1:1-8	1:9-18	1:19-27
84	2:1-13	2:14-26	3:1-18	4:1-10	4:11-17	5:1-12	5:13-20
85	1 Pet 1:1-2	1:3-4	1:5	1:6-9	1:10-12	1:13-17	1:18-25
86	2:1-3	2:4-8	2:9-17	2:18-25	3:1-13	3:14-22	4:1-6
87	4:7-16	4:17-19	5:1-4	5:5-9	5:10-14	2 Pet 1:1-2	1:3-4
88	1:5-8	1:9-11	1:12-18	1:19-21	2:1-3	2:4-11	2:12-22
89	3:1-6	3:7-9	3:10-12	3:13-15	3:16	3:17-18	1 John 1:1-2
90	1:3-4	1:5	1:6	1:7	1:8-10	2:1-2	2:3-11
91	2:12-14	2:15-19	2:20-23	2:24-27	2:28-29	3:1-5	3:6-10
92	3:11-18	3:19-24	4:1-6	4:7-11	4:12-15	4:16—5:3	5:4-13
93	5:14-17	5:18-21	2 John 1:1-3	1:4-9	1:10-13	3 John 1:1-6	1:7-14
94	Jude 1:1-4	1:5-10	1:11-19	1:20-25	Rev 1:1-3	1:4-6	1:7-11
95	1:12-13	1:14-16	1:17-20	2:1-6	2:7	2:8-9	2:10-11
96	2:12-14	2:15-17	2:18-23	2:24-29	3:1-3	3:4-6	3:7-9
97	3:10-13	3:14-18	3:19-22	4:1-5	4:6-7	4:8-11	5:1-6
98	5:7-14	6:1-8	6:9-17	7:1-8	7:9-17	8:1-6	8:7-12
99	8:13—9:11	9:12-21	10:1-4	10:5-11	11:1-4	11:5-14	11:15-19
100	12:1-4	12:5-9	12:10-18	13:1-10	13:11-18	14:1-5	14:6-12
101	14:13-20	15:1-8	16:1-12	16:13-21	17:1-6	17:7-18	18:1-8
102	18:9—19:4	19:5-10	19:11-16	19:17-21	20:1-6	20:7-10	20:11-15
103	21:1	21:2	21:3-8	21:9-13	21:14-18	21:19-21	21:22-27
104	22:1	22:2	22:3-11	22:12-15	22:16-17	22:18-21	

Week 1 — Day 4   Today's verses

Rom.   That the righteous requirement of the law
8:4   might be fulfilled in us, who do not walk
   according to the flesh but according to
   the spirit.

Gal.   But I say, Walk by the Spirit and you shall
5:16   by no means fulfill the lust of the flesh.

Date

Week 1 — Day 5   Today's verses

Phil.   ...Even now Christ will be magnified in
1:20-21   my body.... For to me, to live is Christ....

4:23   The grace of the Lord Jesus Christ be with
   your spirit.

Gal.   If we live by the Spirit, let us also walk by
5:25   the Spirit.

Date

Week 1 — Day 6   Today's verses

1 Cor.   For even as the body is one and has many
12:12-13   members, yet all the members of the
   body, being many, are one body, so also
   is the Christ. For also in one Spirit we
   were all baptized into one Body, whether
   Jews or Greeks, whether slaves or free,
   and were all given to drink one Spirit.

Date

Week 1 — Day 1   Today's verses

Eph.   Predestinating us unto sonship through
1:5   Jesus Christ to Himself, according to the
   good pleasure of His will.

John   In that day you will know that I am in My
14:20   Father, and you in Me, and I in you.

Date

Week 1 — Day 2   Today's verses

Eph.   And He subjected all things under His
1:22-23   feet and gave Him to be Head over all
   things to the church, which is His Body,
   the fullness of the One who fills all in all.

Col.   ...Holding the Head, out from whom all
2:19   the Body, being richly supplied and knit
   together by means of the joints and
   sinews, grows with the growth of God.

Date

Week 1 — Day 3   Today's verses

Rom.   The Spirit Himself witnesses with our
8:16   spirit that we are children of God.

1 Cor.   But he who is joined to the Lord is one
6:17   spirit.

Date

Week 2 — Day 4 | Today's verses

Rom. For as many as are led by the Spirit of
8:14-15 God, these are sons of God. For you have not received a spirit of slavery *bringing you* into fear again, but you have received a spirit of sonship in which we cry, Abba, Father!

14:17 For the kingdom of God is not eating and drinking, but righteousness and peace and joy in the Holy Spirit.

Date

Week 2 — Day 5 | Today's verses

1 Cor. For even as the body is one and has many
12:12 members, yet all the members of the body, being many, are one body, so also is the Christ.

Rom. Do not be slothful in zeal, *but* be burning
12:11 in spirit, serving the Lord.

Date

Week 2 — Day 6 | Today's verses

Rom. For if we, being enemies, were recon-
5:10 ciled to God through the death of His Son, much more we will be saved in His life, having been reconciled.

16:16 ...All the churches of Christ greet you.

14:19 So then let us pursue the things of peace and the things for building up one another.

15:3 For Christ also did not please Himself, but as it is written, "The reproaches of those who reproached You fell upon Me."

Date

Week 2 — Day 1 | Today's verses

Rom. That the righteous requirement of the law
8:4 might be fulfilled in us, who do not walk according to the flesh but according to the spirit.

9 But you are not in the flesh, but in the spirit, if indeed the Spirit of God dwells in you....

16 The Spirit Himself witnesses with our spirit that we are children of God.

Date

Week 2 — Day 2 | Today's verses

Rom. And do not be fashioned according to
12:2 this age, but be transformed by the renewing of the mind that you may prove what the will of God is, that which is good and well pleasing and perfect.

4-5 For just as in one body we have many members, and all the members do not have the same function, so we who are many are one Body in Christ, and indi- vidually members one of another.

Date

Week 2 — Day 3 | Today's verses

Rom. ...We serve in newness of spirit and not
7:6 in oldness of letter.

5:17 ...Much more those who receive the abundance of grace and of the gift of righteousness will reign in life through the One, Jesus Christ.

1:9 For God is my witness, whom I serve in my spirit...

Date

Week 3 — Day 4

Today's verses

1 Cor. 7:10, 12 But to the married I charge, not I but the Lord... But to the rest I say, I, not the Lord...

25 Now concerning virgins I have no commandment of the Lord, but I give *my* opinion as one who has been shown mercy by the Lord to be faithful.

40 But she is more blessed if she so remains, according to my opinion; but I think that I also have the Spirit of God.

_____
Date

Week 3 — Day 5

Today's verses

1 Cor. 1:30 But of Him you are in Christ Jesus, who became wisdom to us from God: both righteousness and sanctification and redemption.

12:13 For also in one Spirit we were all baptized into one Body, whether Jews or Greeks, whether slaves or free, and were all given to drink one Spirit.

15:45 ...The last Adam *became* a life-giving Spirit.

_____
Date

Week 3 — Day 6

Today's verses

1 Cor. 10:17 Seeing that there is one bread, we who are many are one Body; for we all partake of the one bread.

12:12 For even as the body is one and has many members, yet all the members of the body, being many, are one body, so also is the Christ.

Col. 2:19 ...Holding the Head, out from whom all the Body... grows with the growth of God.

_____
Date

Week 3 — Day 1

Today's verses

1 John 4:15 Whoever confesses that Jesus is the Son of God, God abides in him and he in God.

John 15:4-5 Abide in Me and I in you. As the branch cannot bear fruit of itself unless it abides in the vine, so neither *can* you unless you abide in Me. I am the vine; you are the branches. He who abides in Me and I in him, he bears much fruit; for apart from Me you can do nothing.

_____
Date

Week 3 — Day 2

Today's verses

1 Cor. 6:17, 19-20 But he who is joined to the Lord is one spirit....Or do you not know that your body is a temple of the Holy Spirit within you, whom you have from God, and you are not your own? For you have been bought with a price. So then glorify God in your body.

_____
Date

Week 3 — Day 3

Today's verses

1 Cor. 1:9 God is faithful, through whom you were called into the fellowship of His Son, Jesus Christ our Lord.

10:3-4 And all ate the same spiritual food, and all drank the same spiritual drink; for they drank of a spiritual rock which followed *them*, and the rock was Christ.

12:3 Therefore I make known to you that no one speaking in the Spirit of God says, Jesus *is* accursed; and no one can say, Jesus *is* Lord! except in the Holy Spirit.

_____
Date

Week 4 — Day 1

Today's verses

Eph. 4:21 If indeed you have heard Him and have been taught in Him as the reality is in Jesus.

John 14:17 Even the Spirit of reality, whom the world cannot receive, because it does not behold Him or know Him; but you know Him, because He abides with you and shall be in you.

Acts 16:7 ...When they had come to Mysia, they tried to go into Bithynia, yet the Spirit of Jesus did not allow them.

Date

Week 4 — Day 2

Today's verses

Eph. 1:17 That the God of our Lord Jesus Christ, the Father of glory, may give to you a spirit of wisdom and revelation in the full knowledge of Him.

3:3-4 That by revelation the mystery was made known to me, as I have written previously in brief, by which, in reading it, you can perceive my understanding in the mystery of Christ.

Date

Week 4 — Day 3

Today's verses

Eph. 1:18-19 The eyes of your heart having been enlightened, that you may know what is the hope of His calling, and what are the riches of the glory of His inheritance in the saints, and what is the surpassing greatness of His power toward us who believe, according to the operation of the might of His strength.

1 Pet. 1:3 Blessed be the God and Father of our Lord Jesus Christ, who according to His great mercy has regenerated us unto a living hope through the resurrection of Jesus Christ from the dead.

Date

Week 4 — Day 4

Today's verses

Eph. 1:18 ...You may know...what are the riches of the glory of His inheritance in the saints.

2 Cor. 3:3 Since you are being manifested that you are a letter of Christ ministered by us, inscribed not with ink but with the Spirit of the living God; not in tablets of stone but in tablets of hearts of flesh.

Date

Week 4 — Day 5

Today's verses

Eph. 1:13-14 In whom you also, having heard the word of the truth, the gospel of your salvation, in Him also believing, you were sealed with the Holy Spirit of the promise, who is the pledge of our inheritance unto the redemption of the acquired possession, to the praise of His glory.

4:30 And do not grieve the Holy Spirit of God, in whom you were sealed unto the day of redemption.

Date

Week 4 — Day 6

Today's verses

Eph. 1:19-23 And what is the surpassing greatness of His power toward us who believe, according to the operation of the might of His strength, which He caused to operate in Christ in raising Him from the dead and seating Him at His right hand in the heavenlies, far above all rule and authority and power and lordship and every name that is named not only in this age but also in that which is to come; and He subjected all things under His feet and gave Him to be Head over all things to the church, which is His Body, the fullness of the One who fills all in all.

Date

Week 5 — Day 1 — Today's verses

Eph. 2:22 In whom you also are being built together into a dwelling place of God in spirit.

2 Tim. 4:22 The Lord be with your spirit. Grace be with you.

Date

Week 5 — Day 2 — Today's verses

Gen. 28:12 And he dreamed that there was a ladder set up on the earth, and its top reached to heaven; and there the angels of God were ascending and descending on it.

18 And Jacob rose up early in the morning and took the stone that he had put under his head, and he set it up as a pillar and poured oil on top of it.

Heb. 4:16 Let us therefore come forward with boldness to the throne of grace that we may receive mercy and find grace for timely help.

Date

Week 5 — Day 3 — Today's verses

Heb. 9:3-4 And after the second veil, a tabernacle, which is called the Holy of Holies, having a golden altar and the Ark of the Covenant covered about with gold everywhere, in which were the golden pot that had the manna and Aaron's rod that budded and the tablets of the covenant.

10:22 Let us come forward to *the Holy of Holies*...

Date

Week 5 — Day 4 — Today's verses

Eph. 1:17 That the God of our Lord Jesus Christ, the Father of glory, may give to you a spirit of wisdom and revelation in the full knowledge of Him.

3:16 That He would grant you, according to the riches of His glory, to be strengthened with power through His Spirit into the inner man.

Heb. 12:9 ...Shall we not much more be in subjection to the Father of spirits and live?

Date

Week 5 — Day 5 — Today's verses

Eph. 3:17 That Christ may make His home in your hearts through faith...

John 14:23 Jesus...said to him, If anyone loves Me, he will keep My word, and My Father will love him, and We will come to him and make an abode with him.

Matt. 13:23 But the one sown on the good earth, this is he who hears the word and understands, who by all means bears fruit and produces, one a hundredfold, and one sixtyfold, and one thirtyfold.

Date

Week 5 — Day 6 — Today's verses

Eph. 3:19-21 And to know the knowledge-surpassing love of Christ, that you may be filled unto all the fullness of God. But to Him who is able to do superabundantly above all that we ask or think, according to the power which operates in us, to Him be the glory in the church and in Christ Jesus unto all the generations forever and ever. Amen.

Week 6 — Day 4 **Today's verses**

Eph. Husbands, love your wives even as Christ
5:25-27 also loved the church and gave Himself
up for her that He might sanctify her,
cleansing *her* by the washing of the water
in the word, that He might present the
church to Himself glorious, not having
spot or wrinkle or any such things, but
that she would be holy and without
blemish.

Date

Week 6 — Day 5 **Today's verses**

Eph. And receive the helmet of salvation and
6:17-18 the sword of the Spirit, which *Spirit* is the
word of God, by means of all prayer and
petition, praying at every time in spirit
and petition, and watching unto this in all persever-
ance and petition concerning all the
saints.

Date

Week 6 — Day 6 **Today's verses**

Eph. For our wrestling is not against blood and
6:12-13 flesh but against the rulers, against the
authorities, against the world-rulers of
this darkness, against the spiritual *forces*
of evil in the heavenlies. Therefore take
up the whole armor of God...
17-18 And receive the helmet of salvation and
the sword of the Spirit, which *Spirit* is the
word of God, by means of all prayer and
petition...

Date

Week 6 — Day 1 **Today's verses**

Rom. And do not be fashioned according to
12:2 this age, but be transformed by the
renewing of the mind that you may prove
what the will of God is, that which is
good and well pleasing and perfect.
Eph. ...Be renewed in the spirit of your mind.
4:23

Date

Week 6 — Day 2 **Today's verses**

2 Cor. Therefore we do not lose heart; but
4:16 though our outer man is decaying, yet
our inner *man* is being renewed day by
day.
Eph. This therefore I say and testify in the Lord,
4:17 that you no longer walk as the Gentiles
also walk in the vanity of their mind.
23 And *that* you be renewed in the spirit of
your mind.

Date

Week 6 — Day 3 **Today's verses**

Eph. And do not be drunk with wine, in which
5:18-21 is dissoluteness, but be filled in spirit,
speaking to one another in psalms and
hymns and spiritual songs, singing and
psalming with your heart to the Lord,
giving thanks at all times for all things in
the name of our Lord Jesus Christ to *our*
God and Father, being subject to one
another in the fear of Christ.
3:19 And to know the knowledge-surpassing
love of Christ, that you may be filled unto
all the fullness of God.

Date